Perspectives on
Landscape and Settlement
in Nineteenth Century
Ontario

Perspectives on Landscape and Settlement in Nineteenth Century Ontario

edited by

J. David Wood

The Carleton Library No. 91

*Published by Macmillan of Canada Limited
in association with the Institute of
Canadian Studies at Carleton University*

FC
3061
W6 / 28,759

Copyright © The Macmillan Company of Canada Limited 1978

First published by *The Canadian Publishers*
McClelland and Stewart Ltd., 1975

Reprinted by The Macmillan Company of Canada Limited, 1978

ISBN 0-7705-1760-9

Printed in Canada for
The Macmillan Company of Canada Limited
70 Bond Street
Toronto, Ontario
M5B 1X3

Table of Contents

List of Figures

PREFACE

> The country which has founded and maintained these Colonies at a vast expense of blood and treasure, may justly expect its compensation in turning their unappropriated resources to the account of its own redundant population; they are the rightful patrimony of the English people. . . . (Lord Durham's *Report*, 1839)

It would have been a small proportion of the population of Upper Canada which would have felt comfortable with Durham's declaration, in many cases because the majority did not consider themselves really "English" and did not fully accept Imperial domination, in other cases because their interests stood to prosper more without the undue attention of a "mother country". This is not to deny that there was an English—British, to be more correct—presence in Upper Canada. In fact, Durham identified as one of the ingredients of the unrest of the 1830s a tory establishment, British by birth or recent descent. Durham's analysis of Upper Canada was hasty and on some points misguided, but there is no doubt that an influential minority group, drawing its socio-political principles from Old Country conservatism, did flourish through the first half of the century. From the semi-military administrations of the first years through the Family Compact era, the British influence made indelible marks on the province. Some of these marks, which ranged from forms of government and law to details of vernacular architecture, still can be discerned. But, there were other forces afoot in Upper Canada and, whereas it might be said that the War of 1812 served to re-inforce the British connection, the rebelliousness of 1837 was an early step in the breaking of that connection. Upper Canada was a colony not only of Britain, in the political terms in which Durham comprehended it, but increasingly during the nineteenth century an economic and cultural colony of the United States. These forms of colonization involved not merely political subordination (*i.e.*, to Britain) but also value systems and financial gain. Ontario's history has been infused with the discomfort of these contending allegiances. This bipartite colonial condition appears in various guises in the essays herein, and some of its implications are traced.

Southern Ontario has had bestowed on it, like the Canadian plains and some other regions of North America, "a plethora of regional names".[1] Changes in a region's name quite often imply modifications in its boundaries. The area embodied in Southern Ontario, however, while changing its name has remained a fairly stable geographical entity, probably because of its clear-cut peninsular form. The territory embraced within the present book is entirely south of the Algonquin Park highland (see Figure 1.1, which displays place-names applicable to the book as a whole). The various essays are assembled around the general theme of comparisons and contrasts in settlement, and in most cases the area covered is a by-product of the topic. The organization allows the essays to augment one another while not superimposing uniformity. There are a few terms, however, which are common currency and require comment.

"Upper Canada" was the political jurisdiction during most of the time span of the essays. It existed from 1791 (by The Constitutional Act) to 1841 (by The Act of Union), and occupied peninsular Ontario as we now know it as well as stretching into northern Ontario. The name Canada West, which applied to the colony between 1841 and 1867, was not thoroughly accepted and "Upper Canada" continued to be used: witness The Board of Trade of Upper Canada—a title maintained through the 1850s—or, even in some official sources, *The Census of Upper Canada, 1851-52.*[2] A further definition of the territory of the book should clarify that all the essays in Part I have a subject matter that is representative of most parts of Upper Canada, whereas Part II is focussed on south-central Upper Canada from just east of Kingston to the Grand River valley on the west (see Figure 1.1). Part I deals with what we call in places the first generation of ex-European settlement (to the 1840s), although Konrad obviously addresses himself to an earlier period while Kelly, in contrast, looks forward to the formalization of the agricultural scene and Head to the spread of the timber search onto the Shield. The more localized case studies in Part II have more variable time spans, extending to a century in the Osborne paper on Kingston.

The present essays will be found to be more specialized and detailed than their distinguished geographical precursors. Whereas works like Schott's *Landnahme und Kolonisation* and J. D. Rogers' historical geography of Canada were broad, pioneering contributions, and Watson's strongly historical regional geography surveyed the past and presented a number of fruitful models, none had the benefit of the many interpretations of nineteenth century Ontario that have appeared in the past fifteen years. The present essays isolate a single theme and in considerable detail give evidence of the current burgeoning research in the historical geography of Ontario. Even the classic *Urban Development in South-central Ontario*, by Spelt, is taken to the next level of resolution in the essays by Osborne and Ennals. The 1972 monograph on Ontario, edited by Louis Gentilcore, the recent historical geography of Canada by Harris and Warkentin, Warkentin's perceptive Western view of Ontario, and Harris' fundamental survey of Canadian historical geography, have drawn attention to many promising themes which will enrich the agenda for ongoing research.[3] The fact remains, however, that despite increased activity only a modest amount of interpretation of early Ontario has been published by historical geographers.

If one contemplates the man/land relationship in nineteenth century Ontario, normally it is in the currency of the great "geographical historians" who established and extended the Laurentian school of historical writing. The major geographical ideas are represented by the Empire of the St Lawrence, the influences of the Shield, the original ubiquity of commercial forest, Ontario's peninsular situation, and so on. These are images which were being formulated at the end of the nineteenth century, and one or more of them appeared in the writings of Siegfried, Rogers and Newbigin. But they were refined and enriched by the Laurentian historians, and have become a major part of the intellectual setting within which this book originated. Inasmuch as the geographer is concerned with the collaboration of man and nature—in the bestowing of characteristics on places and in the breathing of life into the varied spatial relationships—he is unlikely to make the distinction proffered by Lower, in *Canadians in the Making* (p. xv), between "what man does to his environment" (economic history) and "what his environment does to man" (social history). The traditional debate in historical geography, over the propriety of the "vertical or chronological" vs the "horizontal or cross-sectional" orientation of inquiry, is answered herein through practice. There may be a slight emphasis in Part I on the cross-section and in Part II on the vertical theme, but by and large there is a subtle intertwining of the two, all in the service of the most effective pursuit of the inquiry. The research questions broached in the present volume can be seen to relate to most of the major topics raised by Harris in 1967 (above). There are, of course, many other questions and research designs waiting in the wings, but perhaps this volume at least provides a "portolan chart" for a historical geography of Upper Canada.

The route leading to this publication was laid out some time prior to August 1972, in which month the contributors met with participants in a symposium of the 22nd International Geographical Congress (Settlement Contrasts in the Historical Development of Southern Ontario). Since those stimulating days of discussion, field observation, and peregrination, some of the papers have been lost among other responsibilities while others have been added. The presentation has shifted somewhat from being directed to overseas visitors who knew a lot about settlement geography but little about nineteenth century Ontario, to being suitable for an audience familiar with Ontario history and inquisitive about the frontier as lived out in this part of America. We have made a point of encouraging further inquiry by providing in the Epilogue a basic bibliography under specific topics.

It is not possible today—and probably never has been—to write a book without being indebted to many "Templars" along the way. We are thankful for the noble efforts of unsung heroes in our respective university libraries, and in the Public Archives of Ontario, the Public Archives of Canada, and the Metropolitan Toronto Central Library, as well as in the ranks of departmental secretaries; among the latter, special thanks are due Mrs. Elaine Yates, Atkinson College, York University. We are indebted for the cartography primarily to Christopher Grounds, Atkinson College. It is pleasant to recall the fine scholarly company of the symposium participants and to thank them, not least for giving the contributing Ontario historical geographers cause for coming together. The editor wishes to recognize, finally, the assistance of his colleague, James Cameron, both as co-organizer of the symposium and as a constructive critic of a late draft of parts of this book.

We are pleased to acknowledge financial assistance toward preparation of the symposium and a generous publication grant from the Canadian Committee for Geography.

David Wood,
York University.

Notes

[1] See B. Kaye and D.W. Moodie, "Geographical Perspectives on the Canadian Plains", *in* Richard Allen (ed.), *A Region of the Mind/Interpreting the Western Canadian Plains*, Canadian Plains Studies No. 1 (Regina: University of Saskatchewan, 1973), p. 17.

[2] "Upper Canada" appears in Imperial legislation in 1849: see George W. Spragge, "The Districts of Upper Canada, 1788-1849", *Ontario History*, XXXIX (1947), p.100.

[3] Carl Schott, *Landnahme und Kolonisation in Canada am Beispiel Südontarios* (Geographischen Instituts der Universitat Kiel, Band VI, 1936). J. D. Rogers, *A History of the British Colonies* (ed. by C.P. Lucas), vol. V/ *Canada - Part III/Geographical* (Oxford: Clarendon, 1909). J. Wreford Watson, *North America/Its Countries and Regions* (London: Longmans Green, 1963). Jacob Spelt, *Urban Development in South-central Ontario* (Assen: Van Gorcum, 1955) (reprinted, Carleton Library, No. 57, 1972). Louis Gentilcore (ed.), *Ontario*, Studies in Canadian Geography (University of Toronto Press, 1972). R. Cole Harris and John Warkentin, *Canada Before Confederation/A Study in Historical Geography* (New York: Oxford University Press, 1974). John Warkentin, "Southern Ontario: a View From the West", *The Canadian Geographer*, x (Fall 1966), pp 157-171. R. Colebrook Harris, "Historical Geography in Canada", *The Canadian Geographer*, XI (1967), pp 235-250.

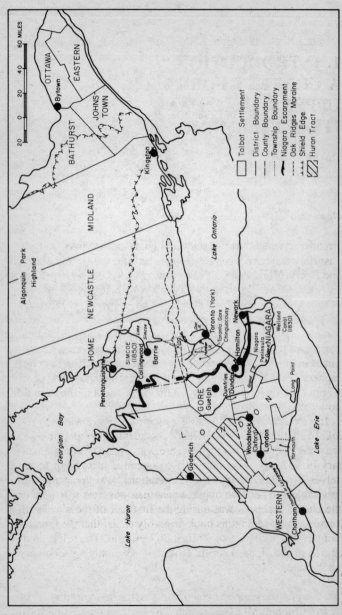

1.1   Southern Ontario: general map of place-names.

1. INTRODUCTION: A CONTEXT FOR UPPER CANADA AND ITS SETTLEMENT

David Wood

Upper Canada and the North Atlantic Triangle

Brebner's famous North Atlantic Triangle can be visualized as a vast flow diagram. The apexes were Britain, the United States, and British North America. The flows for Brebner were primarily financial and diplomatic, but there is no doubt that he thought of the triangle as dynamic, embracing phenomena like the flows of people, commodities, ideas and technology.[1] It is these aspects, assembled into the personalities of places, the varied communications between them, and the human occupance regimes involved, which particularly arrest the attention of geographers. This book is written by historical geographers all of whom have research territory within the segment of the triangle now called Ontario.

It is evident that the flows were reciprocal: there was *give* and *take* in all three directions. Brebner noted that "competition was the order of the day, but the three areas proved to be complementary in so many ways that they co-operated in spite of themselves" (p. 230). Canada's co-operation, however, was even less subject to her own management than was true of Britain or the United States. It was during the first half of the nineteenth century, with which this book primarily deals, that the foundations of this persistent subordination were laid. The select committee of the Upper Canada House of Assembly, in February 1838, said,

. . . by far the greatest objection . . . is, the impossibility . . . of any Colonial Minister, unaided by persons possessing local knowledge, becoming acquainted with the wants, wishes, feelings, and prejudices of the inhabitants of the Colonies, during his temporary continuance in office, and of deciding satisfactorily upon the conflicting statements and claims that are brought before him . . . But it would be performing more than can be reasonably expected from human sagacity, if any man, or set of men, should always decide in an unexceptionable manner on subjects that have their origin thousands of miles from the seat of the Imperial Government, where they reside, and of which they have no personal knowledge whatever. . . .

And Lord Durham's report commented on "this system of irresponsible government" and

. . . the mystery in which the motives and actual purposes of their rulers were hid from the colonists themselves. . . . The Colonies have been frequently the last to learn the things that most concerned them, by the publication of papers on the order of the British Houses of Parliament.[2]

In the nineteenth century North Atlantic give and take, Canada's "giving" was of primary resources, especially timber, as in earlier eras it had been fish and furs. This resource exploitation provided the ingredients for Canada's subordination in the triangle and led to the perennial emphasis on distribution at the expense of production. The major part of the production or processing traditionally has been done outside Canada's boundaries.

Canada's "taking" had two components. Its major component was immigration. In general, the immigrants too came to exploit a primary resource: the cheap, plentiful, and rich land. The balance between immigration and emigration has always been critical for Canada, as it was for early British North America as a whole and for its individual parts. It appears that immigration to British North America, in what was to become a rare occurrence, surpassed the total emigration during the decade prior to 1861.[3] The embryonic Upper Canada opened its doors to settlers in the 1780s. It is estimated that the colony received at least 6,800 and perhaps as many as 10,000

"Loyalists" from the United States in the decade following the successful revolt of the 1770s. This group, however, was a mere vanguard of the millions that would come from across the seas. Of the five million European immigrants who came to North America up to the middle of the nineteenth century, what was to be Ontario received enough to stimulate its population to increase from about 10,000 in 1784 to 952,000 in 1851. In the periods of the late 1820s and late 1840s to mid 1850s, the influx from all sources far exceeded the natural increase, sometimes in a ratio of 2:1. The Canada West censuses of 1848 and 1851-52, faulty though they may be, give an indication of the domesticity of the population. In those years, respectively, 43% and 41% were persons born outside British North America; in both years about 4.5% were persons born in the United States.[4]

The second component of Canada's traditional "taking", one which became deeply rooted during the nineteenth century, was the importation of manufactured products from both Britain and the United States. Fundamentally important goods, like advanced farming and milling machinery, normally were imported. Although there were some improvements locally devised and applied, especially in autochthonous industry, and although there were some minor industrial activities which were suited to local production, such as pottery and simple tool making, yet there was little opportunity for a bullish manufacturing sector to develop in the first half of the nineteenth century.

In many ways British North America's—and in our instance, Upper Canada's—side of the North Atlantic Triangle, although certainly a flow line, is better visualized as a gigantic scale which tipped toward or away from British North America depending on the *weight* placed on it by social or economic conditions at the other two apexes. During certain periods there was an exaggerated tipping of the scale, weighted with emigrants, toward British North America; and there was a consistent tipping of the scale, for certain staple trade commodities, toward Britain.

Crisis in the Old World

The give and take across the North Atlantic was part of a

momentous struggle which was shaking Western society especially in Europe. The *dramatis personae* were The Industrial
Revolution, The Pastoral Tradition, and a political philosophy
distilled into Individualism and *Laissez-faire*. The Industrial
Revolution, aided by its accomplice *Laissez-faire,* was gradually squeezing the life out of the Pastoral Tradition. In brief, an
agriculture-based way of life, which had characterized Europe
in various forms for centuries, was breaking down in the face of
the economic and social demands of burgeoning industry.[5] An
added aggravation was the increase in urban dominance,
through the inexorable concentration of industrial plant and
labour force in urban nuclei, in juxtaposition to the traditional
rural dominance. The casualties, in this politico-economic battle, as one might expect, were those least able to protect themselves: those without flexible skills, those with little or no
education, and those with no savings or property. A large
proportion of the immigration from Britain to British North
America around the turn of the nineteenth century, as a result,
was of people for whom there was little choice, such as the
peasants made redundant by the improving agriculture. In this
period *push* factors predominated. Like the Maritimes, Upper
Canada received some desperate groups, such as the weavers
and other assisted, impoverished, and sickly human cargoes in
the 1820s and 1830s, and most noticeably the Irish in the late
1840s. There are numerous accounts of the Atlantic voyage,
telling of "the crying of children, the swearing of the sailors,
and the scolding of the women", and "fighting, gambling,
riotous or quarrelsome behaviour, swearing and violent language". There were fellow passengers of whom it was said "a
set of greater blackguards never sailed out of England" (1832).[6]
Many of the miserable migrants were subjected to wormy rations, stinking drinking water, and abuse from captain, crew,
and the elements. But enough public information and legislation
had accumulated by the 1820s that Upper Canada also became
the destination of a considerable number of better-informed,
less impoverished immigrants, such as mercenary soldiers,
small farmers, shopkeepers, and clerks.

Differing Cultures in a New Colony

The movement of large numbers of people from advanced culture areas to a developing land raises a debate which is far from concluded: What kinds of preparation did the various cultural groups bring to their life in the New World, and in what ways did they bend the new enviroment to their past experience? It has been satisfactorily demonstrated that settlers who came to Upper Canada with prior North American experience, such as the Loyalists and other Americans, were excellently prepared to occupy their new locations.[7] Indeed, either by design or accident, they often served as leaders in their communities through farming success or initiative in setting up mills, workshops, and other enterprises. It is difficult, on the other hand, to find unequivocal evidence of European immigrants taming their Ontario land in order to adapt it, in anything more than a token way, to the crops and husbandry of their homelands. It certainly is possible to take data from, for instance, the agricultural census returns of 1851 and thereby show districts where perhaps Germans grew more rye, Irish more potatoes, Scots more oats, than their neighbours. Evidence of this kind has been presented by Clark for Prince Edward Island and by Gentilcore for eastern Nova Scotia.[8] It also has been claimed, with reference to Ontario, that

> If I could throw upon a screen here before you a picture of a farm settlement on the St. Lawrence below Brockville, another of a group of farms in the German settlement of Waterloo Co., another of a fruit-growing section between Hamilton and Niagara, another of the Paisley Block in Wellington, another of a French settlement in Essex, you would hardly believe that they all represented different sections of the same province, and you would admit that the origin or nationality of the people had much to do with their condition.[9]

There is little apparent evidence, however, to make one confident that the foregoing Ontario examples are more than ephemeral cases (although some of them still persist). Upper Canadian agriculture seemed to become quickly tied in to the North

American economy and to respond to an environment distinctly more severe than in the European hearthlands. There are too many exceptions, even within a single data source like the agricultural census returns, for one to rest assured with a simple conclusion about such transfer.

One effective way in which old and new worlds were linked was through transhipment of concrete artifacts. Pieces of household and farming equipment, or at least detailed drawings thereof, were brought over by immigrants. One family letter (1837) recommended bringing "the best scythes, pitch forks, spades, graips, adz, hand saw, or any implement that is not heavy". A more ambitious suggestion (1830) was for "a hansom Single horse coup Cart for a patren to the smiths here as they know nothing about Iron exels, nothing being used but Waggons & Sleighs and Great Clumsie ox Carts [sic]".[10] Wives usually would be expected to abandon items of sentiment in favour of those of utility: a decorative bolster in favour of a seive, a family bedstead in favour of a set of carpentry tools, and so on. Bags of seeds were carried over in the settlers' effects, bringing incidentally one of the most *concrete* of imports: alien weed seeds. In another of the Sharp letters referred to above, dated June 2nd, 1821, he expresses a desire for seeds (or the relevant propagule) of rye grass, a particular Scottish potato, the long pod bean, early cabbage, cauliflower, yellow turnip, good oats and barley: "Oates is the poorest trash you ever Saw".

Another way in which the new world reflected old—and perhaps the least adulterated, apart from the elusive traditions of folklore and religious and political mores—was in building. This seldom applied to the first house or barn, which were hasty products of the wilderness. But by the time enough capital had been accumulated to build a permanent homestead, the immigrants commonly set out to enshrine as many of their old country preferences as feasible. Ontario vernacular architecture was blessed with imported styles such as Classical Revival, Regency, Gothic Revival, even Italianate—a colonial reflection of British tastes, to a degree through an American filter. Faithfulness of reproduction was abetted by the influx of old country artisans. Mannion, in a study of Irish settlement in three separate locales in eastern Canada, has demonstrated a highly sophisticated transfer from southern Ireland of design and con-

struction detail in both farm buildings and tools. Such things as
the design of flails and the layout of house hearths appear
indisputably to have come as cultural baggage. It should be
noted, however, that time decay has been much greater in the
economically more vigorous Ontario than in the more stable
study area in Newfoundland's Avalon Peninsula.[11]

Whether or not there was a measurable influence of Old on
New, there was little ambiguity in the general homogenizing
influence of the New World environment on husbandry. Despite
deeply-ingrained practices from the old countries and even the
recording of cases of such practices being employed in Ontario,
a valid generalization is that the new settlers—certainly from the
1790s—were caught up in the Upper Canada agricultural
economy by the time they had struggled through two or three
growing seasons and harvests. There were various ways in
which wheat was superior to any other staple crop—in the
availability of suitable seed, the relative ease of planting in the
"slash and burn" landscape, the simplicity of harvesting, the
possibility of long-term storage, the ease of transport, and the
consistent commercial demand for it. These were New World
economic realities in the first half of the nineteenth century, and
there were few—apart from the pensioned military officers,
called "gentry"—with finances sufficient to struggle against
them. Techniques of husbandry had developed on the strength
of American experience. They were heartily criticized by most
overseas visitors imbued with the imagery of European Agricultural Improvement. The Ontario agricultural scene, in the
pioneering phase, was nothing if not disarrayed. R. L. Jones has
provided a rather notorious characterization of the predominat-
ing North American land-holding group:

. . . they are best described as "land-butchers". They had no
love for well-cleared fields, like the Pennsylvania Dutch, nor
for neatly turned furrows, like many of the British
immigrants.[12]

Such Ontario farmers wasted manure, did not follow scientific
rotations or strive for tidy fields and yards, ignored opportunities to improve their livestock—in short, had little concern
for farming proprieties. In many ways the improvers, re-echoed

by Jones, were right, and before the end of the century Ontario farming was pursuing many of the refinements that were current in European agriculture two generations earlier. But Upper Canadian farming probably was well-suited, as Kelly argues, to the peculiar conditions of a developing territory which, by mid-century, was only beginning to reveal entrenched patterns of internal and external trade, the latter based on two staples.[13] In the face of criticisms by visitors, Upper Canada gained some economic confidence and developed its own style of doing things (similar in the causes of its growth to the more recent Western *modus vivendi* commemorated by Stanley[14]). Its style in agriculture, in summation, appears to have been a successful short-term adaptation to the frontier conditions.

Landscape of Change

Hogs [are] not to run at large . . . [and] no cattle to be free commoners within half a mile of Stores, taverns, mills, or chapels.[15]

The era dealt with in this book embraces the first generation of settlement in Upper Canada, and part of the second. If there is a single revealing criterion of the end of the first generation, of the period of the struggle against the elements and debt, then it is the township by-law represented above. In 1809 it had been declared—and re-iterated at intervening township meetings —that ''hogs shall be free commoners''. Hogs, it is well known, often provided the margin between partial starvation and a sufficient winter food supply, because they were the only meat animal that required no feeding beyond what they could grub for themselves. The restricting by-law, in almost identical wording, can be discovered in minute books from across the province. It occurred at different dates, but whatever the date, its initiation essentially indicated that the district farmers had too many acres in field crops to be willing to tolerate browsing animals running at large and periodically breaking into the crops. The expense of fencing animals in now had become less than the expense of insuring that they were fenced out of the crops. This grass-roots legislation was an early version of the pound by-law which, by the time Saskatchewan and Alberta were settled, was among the first by-laws introduced by an embryonic municipality. In Upper Canada this point usually was reached about twenty years after a continuous, vigorous population increase began.

In insisting on the fencing in of livestock, Upper Canadian farmers were revealing a link at least in principle with the improved agriculture of Western Europe which had promoted enclosure. Perhaps it was an indication of a characteristic never denied—that the aim was commercial agriculture under the banner of the Doctrine of Success. In fact, when one visualizes the *free-hog* landscape of Upper Canada, it is much easier to comprehend why there was such passionate adherence to the free enterprise of the Doctrine of Success (or the Idea of Progress—the European guise) in nineteenth century Ontario. Upward mobility was not only possible; it was necessary! And the Malthusian limits to growth were far from the minds of Upper Canadians. Fencing in was, on the other hand, not only a turning away from the earlier dishevelled landscape but also a turning away from another eligible tradition characteristic of parts of Europe. This was a long-established pastoral tradition, as found among the Highland Scots or in alpine Germany and Switzerland, where the practice was to fence in crops and fence *out* the herded livestock.[16] The resulting scene, as is well known, was fundamentally different. One would not expect, however, to see a society which embraced the Doctrine of Success resting comfortably with a pastoral agriculture.

Rapid change was a trademark of nineteenth century settlement frontiers. In Upper Canada this was expressed in one way through the accumulation of cleared land (that is, land on which trees and underbrush had been cut and burned), at a rate of roughly two to five acres per year on an average active farm. The aggrandizement of towns and villages provided further dramatic evidence of change. A letter written home to Scotland claimed that between 1829 and 1833 Hamilton had tripled and York, Dundas, and Galt had doubled in size; the twenty-five smoking chimneys counted on arrival at Galt had given rise to twenty-five more. And Smith, in his *Gazetteer*, says of London, ''Building . . . [after two major fires] has been proceeded with rapidly; and in place of the old frame buildings, handsome streets have been erected, composed of brick buildings three and four stories high''.[17] This was a period in which a rather dense network of urban nuclei was necessary, to supply the myriad of farms being established in the wilderness, only to undergo a changing of the network scale in the succeeding generation or two.

Change seemed to get into the blood of Upper Canada and aroused in it a spectacular rate of population mobility such as has become a part of the Frontier Idea. Studies such as that by Gagan and Mays, on Toronto Gore township, now are documenting population ingress and egress. Some initial findings show extremely high turnover, especially but not exclusively among householders without land. Gagan and Mays found that in any ten-year period between 1837 and 1881 about half the householders in Toronto Gore moved out.[18] These authors remind us that evidence from both rural and urban jurisdictions in the United States in the nineteenth century indicates high mobility, and specifically with reference to rural areas of the northern mid-West demonstrates a turnover of seventy to eighty per cent of the population during the decades between 1860 and 1890. Evidence dating to the 1840s in assessment rolls for Chinguacousy township, also in Peel County, suggests that a rate approaching eighty per cent is applicable for that decade.[19] A bird's eye view at that time would have shown, in Upper Canada south of a Lake Simcoe-Goderich line, patches of settlement biting into the woodland. There would have been little indication, however, of the geometry that was to dominate the scene by the end of the nineteenth century and, as McIlwraith argues in this book, few of the roads would have been improved and widened enough to break the canopy of leaves. But it appears that under the camouflage there was an abundance of coming and going, a veritable bee-hive of activity. It is that activity and the infrastructure channelling it which this book submits to analysis.

Notes

[1] J.B. Brebner, *North Atlantic Triangle The Interplay of Canada, the United States and Great Britain*, The Carleton Library, No. 30 (Toronto: McClelland & Stewart, 1966; originally 1945).

[2] Both quotations are from C.P. Lucas (ed.), *Lord Durham's Report*

on the Affairs of British North America [1839], 3 volumes (Oxford: The Clarendon Press, 1912), pp. 104-105 & 107 in Vol. II.

[3]W. E. Kalbach & W. W. McVey, *The Demographic Bases of Canadian Society* (Toronto: McGraw-Hill, 1971), ch. 1. See also Helen I. Cowan, *British Emigration to British North America, 1783-1837* [1928] (University of Toronto, rev. ed., 1961).

[4]Canada, Dep't of Agriculture, *Censuses of Canada, 1665 to 1871 . . . Statistics of Canada . . .* , Vol. IV (of 1871 Census) (Ottawa, 1876), pp 166, 182.

[5]Frank Thistlethwaite, "Migration from Europe Overseas in the Nineteenth and Twentieth Centuries", *Rapports*, XI Congrès International des Sciences Historiques (Stockholm, 1960), V, pp 32-60 (quotation, p. 53).

[6]Quoted in Edwin C. Guillet, *The Great Migration/The Atlantic Crossing by Sailing-ship Since 1770*, 2nd ed. (University of Toronto Press, 1963), pp. 66, 69, 5 in supplement.

[7]Kenneth Kelly, "Wheat Farming in Simcoe County in the Mid-nineteenth Century", *Canadian Geographer*, XV (1971), pp 95-112. Gerald M. Craig, *Upper Canada/The Formative Years/1784-1841* (Toronto: McClelland and Stewart, 1963), chapter 1.

[8]Andrew H. Clark, *Three Centuries and the Island, a Historical Geography of Settlement and Agriculture in Prince Edward Island, Canada* (University of Toronto Press, 1959). R. Louis Gentilcore, "The Agricultural Background of Settlement in Eastern Nova Scotia", originally 1956, but revised by the author for his book of readings, *Canada's Changing Geography* (Scarborough: Prentice-Hall, 1967).

[9]Quoted from the *Report of the Ontario Bureau of Industries for 1898*, in R.L. Jones, *History of Agriculture in Ontario/1613-1880* (University of Toronto Press, 1946), p. 51 (footnote 3).

[10]From private letters, the first by Duncan Ferguson, Yarmouth Township, U.C., 30th Sept. 1837, the second by James Sharp, Dumfries Township, U.C., 4th Feb. 1830.

[11]John Mannion, *Irish Settlements in Eastern Canada, A study of cultural transfer and adaptation*, Univ. of Toronto Department of Geography Research Publications, Vol. 12 (1974).

[12]Robert Leslie Jones, *History of Agriculture in Ontario/1613-1880* (University of Toronto Press, 1946), p 53.

[13]Kenneth Kelly, "Wheat Farming in Simcoe . . .", and his chapter in this book. W.A. Macintosh, "Some Aspects of a Pioneering Economy", *Canadian Journal of Economics and Political Science*, II (1936), pp 457-463. D.A. Lawr, "The Development of Ontario Farming, 1870-1914: Patterns of Growth and Change," *Ontario History*, LXIV (1972), pp 239-251.

[14]George F. G. Stanley, "The Western Canadian Mystique", *in* D.

Gagan (ed.), *Prairie Perspectives*, papers of the Western Canadian Studies Conference (Toronto: Holt Rinehart & Winston, 1970), pp 6-27.

[15]From "Proceedings of the township meeting for King . . . 2nd Jan.y 1837", Home District, Upper Canada. Public Archives of Ontario: Gs-mf (LML II-59).

[16]This point owes its existence to a comment by Dr. Wilhelm Matzat, Bonn University, to whom I am thankful.

[17]Private unpublished letter by Walter Cowan, Dumfries Township, 16th Sept. 1833. William H. Smith, *Smith's Canadian Gazetteer Comprising Statistical and General Information Respecting All Parts of the Upper Province, or Canada West* . . . (Toronto, 1846; Coles Canadiana Reprint, 1970), p. 100.

[18]David Gagan and Herbert Mays, "Historical Demography and Canadian Social History: Families and Land in Peel County, Ontario", *Canadian Historical Review*, LIV (Mar. 1973), pp 27-47.

[19]J. David Wood, "Simulating Pre-census Population Distribution", *The Canadian Geographer*, XVIII (Sept. 1974).

Part I:
Geographical Themes
on Nineteenth
Century Ontario

The country all the way [from Hamilton to Brantford] was rich, and beautiful, and fertile beyond description—the roads abominable as could be imagined to exist. . . . I remember a space of about three miles on this road, bordered entirely on each side by dead trees, which had been artificially blasted by fire, or by girdling. . . . If there were but a railroad . . . there is no calculating the advantages that must arise . . . ; but "want of capital", as I hear all around me—and they might add want of energy, want of enterprise, want of everything needful. . . are likely to defer the completion of this magnificent plan for many years. (Anna Jameson, 1837)

The views of Upper Canada by Bartlett, John Howard, or James Hamilton, which depict a manicured scene striving to be like a corner of Europe, do not sit well with the vivacious word portrait above. We must presume either that the artists and the writer were not dealing with the same Canadian subject matter, or that the few months between the paintings and the writing had wrought a remarkable change in the scene, or that there were different expressions of subjectivity at work. The last probably is closest to the truth. Many of the artists whose works have survived were unwitting propagandists for their social class and aesthetic school. (Writers too practised an "acceptable" style, but more contrasting opinions were expressed in the different travel accounts). The subjectivity of the evidence, particularly the visual evidence, lays a burden on the researcher who hopes to discover from such perceptions meaningful aspects of the landscape of the past. Any evidence which can help to corroborate geographical relationships, particularly any that is the result of a careful and replicable search procedure, is to be prized. Evidence of the Indian occupance of southern Ontario generally is of this type, and because the Indians occupied the same territory and pursued an agricultural livelihood, there are many potentially revealing comparisons to be made.

The Ontario Iroquois had maintained an agricultural settlement in southern Ontario for six hundred years before the British government began signing treaties with their successors for parts of the territory. Most of the signs of clearing had been obliterated before the American and British immigrants began filing into Ontario, and there was no awareness that agriculturalists had cleared and cultivated large areas in southwestern and eastern Ontario, the Niagara Peninsula, Huronia, the Collingwood area, and the Toronto area, in some cases within the previous 150 years. Although Konrad pays particular attention to the Toronto area, his paper is general in the sense that he shows many of the prehistorical settlement characteristics to have been common much more widely. One comparison with the historical period is in the practice of agriculture. One contrast is between the village-based character of the Indian settlement and the scattered rural character of ex-European occupance of which a gazetteer said, in 1813: "There are not many villages . . . of much note, the inhabitants finding their greatest advantage in agriculture, as the land is very cheap and fertile."[1] When we consider the Iroquois occupance it becomes obvious that there are alternative man/land relationships and different development priorities to the ones followed by the ambitious pioneers in nineteenth century Ontario.

The settlement that followed Britain's opening of Canada above Montreal to refugees and soldier-settlers was endowed with some clear characteristics. For one thing it was a colony, and it, along with the rest of British North America, became almost a surrogate for the lost American colonies. The way in which Upper Canada was designed and managed was meant to insure against it defecting and indeed to provide a counterbalance to United States influence in the Great Lakes basin. For another thing, the initial settlement came as a flood into accessible border areas, its main impetus arising from the pushing of the Loyalists out of the Republic. The development of the colony from this point to 1851 is sketched out in the Gentilcore and Wood paper, as a prologue to the essays following.

Two things were of primary importance to the "average" rural settler: the success of his struggle to carve out a farm, and the possibility of his communicating with other settlers and the markets. These aspects are dealt with by Kelly and McIlwraith. The discussion of the communication by road is placed in the framework of the farmer on the land. What were the conditions of the early roads, and what experiences might a settler have gone through in getting to mill or market? McIlwraith makes the point that through most of the first generation of settlement the roads, being little more than trails, were relatively unobtrusive in the rural scene; in the words of Mrs. Traill, on the trip to her brother's homestead in 1832, "the road we were on appeared to end in a cedar swamp . . . so . . . we agreed to retrace our steps . . . [but] there was no other road to the lake".[2] In modern terms, the "biomass" obviously was dominant, in striking contrast to the present-day urbanized scene wherein—following Bunge's contention—"machinemass" is dominating and perhaps threatening the life systems.[3] The town, in McIlwraith's description of it, was far from threatening to the farmers of Upper Canada; in fact, it was a linch-pin in the seasonal round of activities. The visit to town usually was a matter for celebration because it meant new supplies, perhaps cash in pocket, news from afar, and often contact with friends or relatives.

Kelly's discussion of the organization of the agricultural scene draws a contrast between the early decades of settlement and the later decades of the nineteenth century. Within the general context of the common wheat-fallow-wheat husbandry, there was a great variety of farming practices, minor crop and animal emphases, and homestead scenes. Kelly's main contribution, however, is to show not the differences but the common aspects of establishing a farm in the forest. He identifies the steps ("man/land stances") from the first swing of the axe through to an established farmer's decision regarding, for example, tile drainage. The multifarious frontier scene, as Kelly goes on to argue, gradually crystallized through an evolutionary sequence of farmscapes into what he refers to as "agricultural landscapes", or agricultural regions.[4] Important influences which began to manifest themselves in the regionalization were the physiological aspects of the land being used for farming.

The exploitation of the timber resource both preceded and accompanied the agricultural invasion. In the Lake Ontario basin and the upper St. Lawrence Valley the search for pine suitable as square timber came a few years after the earliest settlers. It concentrated at first in the lower reaches of the streams, but soon moved further and further into the back country and there provided the beginning farmer with an additional source of income. The demand for square timber outstripped even the demand for agricultural land around mid-century, and as a result the timber exploitation moved ahead of the influx of agricultural settlers into the northern and north-western parts of peninsular Ontario. Statistics on exports shed light on the agriculture/timber comparison in revealing that, during the third to fifth decades of the nineteenth century, timber exports exceeded in value those of agriculture. The timber industry on the Shield is a focus of Head's paper. His detailed study of the Belleville Agency clarifies a number of neglected aspects of the industry. Using evidence from that area, he distinguishes between logging for square timber and for lumber, traces the network of the industry even to the locations and relationships of the camps, and concludes with a model of the hierarchy of points and paths—in effect, the semi-permanent "physical plant"—in a timbershed.

Notes

[1] M[ichael] Smith, *A Geographical View of the Province of Upper Canada and Promiscuous Remarks on the Government.* . . . (New-York: the author, 1813), p. 47.

[2] Catharine Parr Traill, *The Backwoods of Canada*, Selections (by Clara Thomas), New Canadian Library No. 51 (Toronto: McClelland & Stewart, 1971), p. 50.

[3] William W. Bunge, "The Geography of Human Survival", *Annals*, Association of American Geographers, LXIII (Sept. 1973), pp 275-295.

[4] *Cf* Robert L. Jones, *History of Agriculture in Ontario/1613-1880* (University of Toronto Press, 1946); P.W. Bidwell and J.I. Falconer, *History of Agriculture in the Northern United States, 1620-1860*

(Washington: Carnegie Institution, 1925); James T. Lemon, *The Best Poor Man's Country, A Geographical Study of Early Southeastern Pennsylvania* (Baltimore: Johns Hopkins, 1972) (a century earlier but relevant).

2. DISTRIBUTION, SITE AND MORPHOLOGY OF PREHISTORICAL SETTLEMENTS IN THE TORONTO AREA

Victor A. Konrad

Archaeological surveys, carried out in Southern Ontario, indicate concentrations of prehistorical agricultural settlements in Huronia,[1] the Grand River Valley[2] and the Norfolk Sand Plain,[3] to name but a few areas. The spatial characteristics of these site concentrations and the morphology of the agriculture villages themselves have been subjected to a comprehensive geographical interpretation in Huronia alone.[4] Although numerous archaeological surveys, relatively extensive archaeological research in an Ontario context, and a wealth of ethnohistorical documents have allowed the geographical analysis of prehistorical settlement in Huronia, only now are comprehensive archaeological surveys and salvage archaeology presenting us with glimpses of the prehistorical settlement characteristics of the Toronto area.

The present study investigates the distribution of prehistorical village sites in the Toronto area and also examines the changing environmental and morphological characteristics of the prehistorical Ontario Iroquois settlement.

The Ontario Iroquois village, not unlike the Neolithic village of the Old World, was diachronically far removed from the agricultural village that developed from European settlement of the Toronto area about the turn of the 19th Century. Although the times of occupance were only separated by two hundred to nine hundred years, they might as well have been separated by two thousand years. Prehistorical settlement was the precursor of ex-European settlement, but there the connection ends. A number of interesting comparisons, however, can be made between the two. A few aspects of comparison between indigenous and ex-European agricultural settlement in the area are treated briefly at the end of this paper, primarily as a connection to papers that follow in this volume.

The Distribution of Prehistorical Village Sites

A recent, comprehensive survey of the archaeological sites in the Metropolitan Toronto area provides detailed information on the location, size and physical characteristics of the sites.[5] Although sufficient artifactual material is not yet available to assign all of the 191 sites located to a place in the cultural chronology, all of the *village* sites can be affiliated with at least an archaeological time period. A substantial amount of archaeological excavation will be required to refine the chronology for the area.

The distribution of sites appears as Figure 2.1. Prehistorical village sites are those affiliated with the Initial Woodland and Terminal Woodland periods only. Laurentian Archaic peoples, who occupied the river valleys of the Toronto area between 5000 B.C. and 1000 B.C. were not agriculturalists. "An examination of the discarded food bones from sites suggest that the Laurentian people were predominantly big game hunters who relied mainly on such animals as deer, elk, bear and beaver. Smaller game animals, fish, shell-fish, and wild plant foods were also used but they appear to have supplemented the big game diet."[6] Only one dart head, diagnostic of the Palaeo-Indian Period (about 9000-5000 B.C.), has been found in the Toronto area.[7] The Palaeo-Indians, who were also big game hunters, followed the caribou and may have hunted such extinct Pleistocene mammals as the mammoth and the mastodon.[8] A number of historical Indian sites are also recorded in Figure 2.1. They are either Historic Iroquois villages or Historic Mississauga camps or villages. After the destruction of Huronia,[9] the Iroquois Confederation (or New York State Iroquois) conquered most of southern Ontario. In the Toronto area, their large villages, "Teyagon" near the mouth of the Humber River and "Ganestiquiagon" near the mouth of the Rouge River, controlled the portage routes to Lake Simcoe.[10] Agricultural settlement during the historical period was disrupted by the fur trade and the influence of French missions, and as such will not

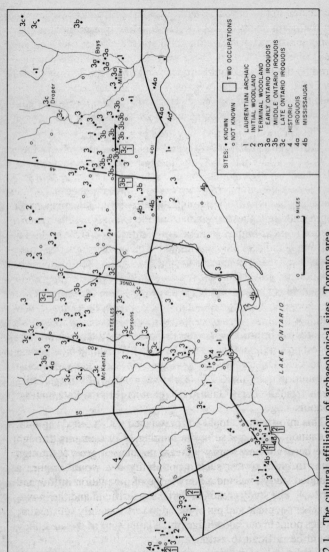

2.1 The cultural affiliation of archaeological sites, Toronto area.

be treated in this paper. After the demise of Iroquois settlement on the north shore of Lake Ontario, Mississauga Indians (Algonquian hunters and gatherers from the shores of Georgian Bay) filled the vacuum. These were the native peoples encountered by the Loyalist and European settlers to the Toronto area. By 1806, all of the Indian lands in the area had been purchased and the Mississaugas were left with a number of small reserves.[11] Here they subsisted on hunting, gathering and some agriculture.

Figure 2.2 provides a representation of the percentage (cumulative adjusted frequency) of Toronto area sites that are affiliated with the recognized divisions of the cultural chronology. The lower graph represents all of the sites in Figure 2.1 that have been assigned to some cultural affiliation. The upper graph represents only those sites that have been assigned to specific archaeological stages. For example, although all of the Terminal Woodland sites are represented in the lower graph, they have not all been identified as Early Ontario Iroquois, Middle Ontario Iroquois or Late Ontario Iroquois. Only those sites identified with these affiliations appear in the upper graph. The majority of the Toronto sites are Woodland sites. Although only a few Initial Woodland sites were located, approximately 55% of all the sites can be attributed to the Terminal Woodland period. The largest proportion of the tested Terminal Woodland sites appear to be Late Ontario Iroquois villages. In fact, the percentage distribution in Figure 2.2 points to an increase of village settlements from the Early Ontario Iroquois stage to the Late Ontario Iroquois stage.

This information should be approached with a certain amount of caution. An increase in the number of settlements through time need not necessarily indicate population growth through time. In order to test such a possibility one would require a bounded study area and a knowledge of population inflow and outflow. The study area boundaries are artificial and the movements of people in and out of the area were certainly substantial. At this point in our knowledge of the prehistory of the area, they would be difficult to estimate.

Wright, in his *Ontario Iroquois Tradition*,[12] suggests that the Ontario Iroquois occupied different parts of southern Ontario between 1000 and 1600 A.D. The archaeological evidence indicates that the Early Ontario Iroquois developed *in situ* from

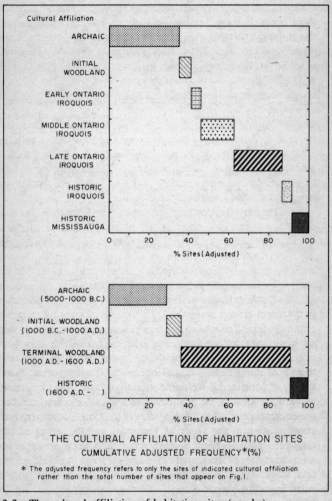

Cultural Affiliation

ARCHAIC

INITIAL WOODLAND

EARLY ONTARIO IROQUOIS

MIDDLE ONTARIO IROQUOIS

LATE ONTARIO IROQUOIS

HISTORIC IROQUOIS

HISTORIC MISSISSAUGA

0   20   40   60   80   100
% Sites (Adjusted)

ARCHAIC
(5000-1000 B.C.)

INITIAL WOODLAND
(1000 B.C.-1000 A.D.)

TERMINAL WOODLAND
(1000 A.D.-1600 A.D.)

HISTORIC
(1600 A.D. -   )

0   20   40   60   80   100
% Sites (Adjusted)

THE CULTURAL AFFILIATION OF HABITATION SITES
CUMULATIVE ADJUSTED FREQUENCY*(%)

* The adjusted frequency refers to only the sites of indicated cultural affiliation
rather than the total number of sites that appear on Fig. I.

2.2   The cultural affiliation of habitation sites (graphs).

an Initial Woodland base in southwestern Ontario.[13] One branch (Pickering Culture) of the Early Ontario Iroquois moved to the north shore of Lake Ontario, while the other (Glen Meyer Culture) remained in southwestern Ontario. "The Middle Ontario Iroquois stage is a product of the uninterrupted cultural development of the Pickering Branch and the conquest and absorption of the Glen Meyer branch by the Pickering branch."[14] During this stage, between about 1300 and 1400 A.D., village settlements were located throughout most of southern Ontario. The Late Ontario Iroquois stage again saw the concentration of village sites in specific portions of southern Ontario. Late Ontario Iroquois peoples, living in the area north of Lake Ontario, moved to the southern shore of Georgian Bay where they became the Huron and Petun of historical times. In southwestern Ontario, they moved to the north shore of Lake Erie, the Grand River valley and the Niagara Frontier and became known as the Neutral and Erie.

Evidence to support the theory of Ontario Iroquois development is apparent in the distribution of sites (Figure 2.1). All of the stages are represented by a complement of sites. In addition, the concentratons of earlier sites appear to be discrete. Almost all of the Early Ontario Iroquois sites are located in one concentration, a concentration that contains no óther sites. Most of the Middle Ontario Iroquois sites also appear in one concentration in the upper Rouge watershed. This group of sites is comprised of mostly Middle Ontario Iroquois settlements but also contains a few villages that are associated with the Late Ontario Iroquois stage. Discrete concentrations are more likely to support a theory of movements, in and out of the Toronto area, than a theory of localized development through time. The occurrence of the Late sites in the Middle Ontario Iroquois concentration, the occurrence of a few Middle sites in the Late Ontario Iroquois concentration in the Town of Vaughan, and the *string* of Late sites across the northern portion of the study area, are all in line with the theory of Iroquoian development from the Middle to the Late stage. The Ontario Iroquois, during the Late stage, moved west from the upper Rouge watershed occupied during the Middle stage, to the upper Humber River valley and the Black Creek area. The Middle stage settlements in Vaughan could be forerunners of a major move during the transition period. In fact, their location in the Town of Vaughan suggests that the move probably took place about 1400 A.D. According to the theory, Ontario Iroquois peoples from eastern Ontario moved west to join others, already in the Humber River valley, prior to their move to northern Simcoe County. The Late stage settlements, located in northern Pickering Township, tend to support this hypothesis. The move to Huronia has been studied by Dr. J.N. Emerson of the University of Toronto. His excavations of a number of sites in the Black Creek area and in the upper Humber valley have provided evidence of a decrease in the age of sites from south to north.[15]

Although evidence to support the theory of Ontario Iroquois development is apparent in the spatial distribution of sites, this is by no means conclusive. A considerable number of sites will require excavation before the theory can be substantiated. Ontario Iroquois settlements located in the upper Rouge and in the Town of Vaughan should receive excavation priority.

The Prehistorical Village Site

Geographical analysis of the distribution of prehistorical villages in the Toronto area can provide little more than a preliminary explanation of Ontario Iroquois movements. In view of the exploratory nature of most of the archaeological excavation in the area, the basic cultural affiliation data required for the execution of distributional analyses, similar to those carried out by Newcomb in his studies of Iron Age settlement in Cornwall,[16] are not available. Site data are available for the Toronto area villages and an analysis of these data can provide valuable insights into the relationships between the village and the immediate physical environment.[17] These relationships can be translated as village site requirements.

The Ontario Iroquois were shifting cultivators who moved their settlements from three to six miles[18] from the old site every eight to twelve years.[19] The reasons given for the move by Sagard and the Jesuits were both soil and firewood depletion.[20] Heidenreich suggest that fields were progressively cleared further away from the village site as the land in proximity to the village was depleted. Eventually the distance to the fields would become prohibitive and the village would be forced to relocate.[21]

As shifting cultivators, the Ontario Iroquois kept a number of specific site factors in mind in their search for a location to settle. "To the Huron the selection of a village site was anything but a haphazard affair. As a matter of fact considerable care seems to have been exercised in this regard. Each site had to have a combination of specific requirements among which proximity to a source of water, a hinterland of arable soils, an available source of firewood, proximity to a young secondary forest and a defendable position seem to have been the most important".[22] The site requirements of the Ontario Iroquois in the Toronto area could not have been drastically different.

A glance at Figure 2.1 suggests that most of the Terminal Woodland settlements were located close to sources of water. This visual impression is, however, inadequate. During the archaeological survey of the Metropolitan Toronto area, detailed information was recorded for the following environmental characteristics: drainage, slope, distance to nearest water source, type of nearest water source, and soil texture. The early land surveyor's notebooks[23] were also consulted for information on the pre-settlement vegetation of the area. The rationale for this was to investigate whether the species composition on the sites might reflect any conscious choice by the village occupants. Since a period of approximately 250 years elapsed between the Late Ontario Iroquois occupation and the land survey around Toronto, the effects on the vegetation of the prehistorical agricultural occupance should no longer be readily apparent. It follows that the species composition recorded by the land surveyors may well approximate the forest cleared by the Ontario Iroquois agriculturalists prior to village construction. Heidenreich suggests that "Far more important than any single species or association of species, was the actual size composition of a particular timber stand. Huron technology in coping with large trees was limited, and the nature of the construction of their villages demanded enormous quantities of logs under twelve inches in diameter."[24] Although his theory on size composition cannot be tested for prehistoric Ontario Iroquois sites, the relationship between site and species composition can.

TABLE 2.1

Physical Site Factors and the Location of Ontario Iroquois Villages in the Toronto Area

A. *Drainage*

% of villages	Poorly Drained	Imperfectly Drained	Well Drained
	0.0	12.5	87.5

B. *Type of nearest water source*

% of villages	None	Spring	Stream	River	Lake
	10.3	63.2	21.8	4.6	0.0

C. *Distance to reliable water source* (feet)

% of villages	< 50	50-500	501-1000	1001-5000	>5000
	21.6	61.4	8.0	6.8	2.3

D. *Slope*

% of villages	Level	Gentle (0-5°)	Rolling (6-15°)	Moderately Steep (16-25°)	Steep (>25°)
	0.0	23.9	55.7	20.5	0.0

E. *Vegetation*

% of villages	Oak, Oak and Pine, Grasses	Maple, Oak, Basswood, Pine, Hemlock, Beech	Maple, Basswood, Elm, Beech	Elm, Black Oak, Cedar, Ash	Cedar, Birch, Swamp Vegetation
	20.9	47.7	26.7	4.7	0.0

F. *Soil Texture*

% of villages	Sand	Sandy Loam	Loam	Clay Loam	Clay	Muck
	4.0	38.2	33.3	21.5	3.0	0.0

Sources: *Ontario Soil Survey,* Reports 18, 19 and 23. Ontario Land Surveyor's Notes, 1793-1829. For an Index to these notes see Gentilcore, R. L. and K. Donkin, *Land Surveys of Southern Ontario,* Cartographica Monograph No. 8, 1973. Konrad, *Archaeological Resources of the Metropolitan Toronto Planning Area,* pp. 26-47.

The site requirements of the Ontario Iroquois agriculturalists of the Toronto area are clearly brought out in Table 2.1. Almost all of the villages are located within five hundred feet of a reliable water source. This water source is usually a spring or a stream. Springs were likely preferred because they could insure a reliable, fresh water source for a village's requirements both during the dry summer and the freeze-up of winter. Springs are often found located near breaks in slope rather than on level land. All of the village sites in the Toronto area are found in areas of gentle, rolling or moderately steep slopes. As in the case of the Huron, natural breaks in slope were sought in order to provide the village with a defensible position. The archaeological evidence indicates that palisades were constructed to reinforce the natural defences. Since breaks in slope are often found in association with springs or streams, the preferred location for the Ontario Iroquois settlement appears to have been on an elevated area next to a spring or stream.

But these were not the only site requirements sought by the Indian agriculturalists. From Table 2.1 it appears that they preferred well-drained areas with sandy loam, loam or clay loam soils. The largest proportion of village sites were located in areas that once supported a mixed forest of maple, oak, basswood, pine, hemlock and beech. Villages were also situated in drier areas supporting only oak, pine and grasses, and in wetter areas with a forest of maple, basswood, elm and beech. The vegetation differences seem to reflect minor differences in drainage on the sites rather than a clear preference for any species composition. Table 2.1 indicates that most of the village sites were well-drained. The arboreal vegetation, being sensitive to drainage differences, merely emphasizes minor disparities. This supports Heidenreich's statement that "macrovegetational patterns seem to have no obvious relation to the distribution of village sites."

The distribution of villages in relation to soil texture indicates different situations for Huronia and the Toronto area. While 68.5% of the Huron villages were located on sandy loams, only 38.2% of the Toronto villages appear in association with the same textural class, and a substantial number of villages were also located on loams (33.3%) and clay loams (21.5%). A careful examination of this disparity indicates a possible reason

TABLE 2.2

Terminal Woodland Village Sites in the Toronto Area —
Indices of Preference for Selected Soil Texture Classes

Soil Texture Class	% in Area	Number of Sites	% Sites	INDEX
Loam	21.8	34	33.3	1.5
Sandy Loam	14.6	39	38.2	2.6
Clay Loam	28.4	22	21.5	1.3
Sand	4.4	4	4.0	0.9
Clay	29.2	3	3.0	0.1
Muck	1.6	0	0.0	0.0

(Soil texture data from reports 18, 19 and 23 of the *Ontario Soil Survey*).

for it. Table 2.2 provides the indices of preference (or location quotients) for soil texture, evidenced by the location of Terminal Woodland villages in the Toronto area. The index of preference for a phenomenon relates the percentage of sites on the phenomenon to the percentage of the phenomenon in the total area, thus providing a more accurate evaluation of the concentration of sites in soil texture classes that are not equally represented in terms of area.[25] The index of preference for sandy loam soils is by far the highest at 2.6 since 38.2% of the villages were located on soils that comprise only 14.6% of the area. In Huronia, a total of 68.5% of all village sites were located on sandy loams that cover 40% of the total area[26] and show an index of preference of only 1.7. This in fact indicates that the preference for sandy loam soils was even higher in the Toronto area than in Huronia. These soils, however, were not in as great abundance in the vicinity of Toronto, and the Ontario Iroquois agriculturalists were obliged to locate on other loam soils. Poorly drained clay and muck soils, and also droughty sands were avoided.

An examination of the distribution of village sites in relation to soil texture for the three developmental stages of the Ontario Iroquois period, indicates a preference for only sandy loam soils by the Pickering peoples, a preference for mainly loam soils by the Middle Ontario Iroquois and a preference for both sandy loam and clay loam soils by the Late Ontario Iroquois.[27] Although these changes in preference in part indicate what well-drained soils were available in the respective areas of settlement concentration, they also may indicate a move from areas of sandy loam soils due to population pressure. This may well be the case since almost equal quantities of sandy loam soils are represented in all of the major village concentrations related to a specific substage of the Terminal Woodland. The growth of population is indicated by the increasing size of the villages and the increasing number of settlements through time.[28] To take this one step further, the changes in preference for soil texture may also indicate an adaptation of agricultural technology and cultivated plants to a wider variety of soils through time. Since the cultigens grown by the Ontario Iroquois must have adapted to many soil texture and drainage conditions in their diffusion from Central America to southern Ontario,[29] it seems unlikely that the corn and other vegetables grown by these peoples required a lengthy period of adaptation to the soils of the Toronto area. More likely is the possibility that Ontario Iroquois agricultural technology, developed just prior to the Early Ontario Iroquois stage,[30] required time to develop. At first only the loose sandy loam soils could be cultivated. With the development of agricultural techniques and implements, the more compact loams and clay loams also could be worked.

In summary, the prehistorical villages in the Toronto area were characterized by a number of specific environmental features. Most important among these was a reliable source of water, preferably a spring or stream, in close proximity to the site. The proximity to a stream or spring also insured the requirement of a break in slope for protection. Since they were incipient agriculturalists, the village occupants sought out areas of well-drained sandy loam, loam or clay loam soils for their settlements.

The Developing Prehistorical Village Pattern

Although few Terminal Woodland village sites in the Toronto area have seen even partial excavation, there is evidence to indicate that these settlements were circular in shape, were often palisaded, were up to ten acres in size and contained a number of elongated ovate structures or longhouses. There is also evidence to indicate a development of village pattern, from the Early

Ontario Iroquois stage to the Late Ontario Iroquois stage, ex-
hibiting a growth in settlement size, a growth in longhouse
length, an increase in fortifications and a change in overall
village morphology. This development of village pattern is best
examined by considering examples from the three stages of the
Ontario Iroquois.

Our information for the Early Ontario Iroquois stage is relatively good. Dr. W. Kenyon, of the Royal Ontario Museum, in
his near complete excavation of the Miller site,[31] a Pickering
Culture component near the present day village of Pickering,
has located evidence of a small prehistorical village little more
than an acre in size. This Early Ontario Iroquois settlement is
almost circular and contains at least six house structures varying
in length from 38.1 to 60.1 feet and in breadth from 20.6 to 27.0
feet (Figure 2.3).[32] The entrance appears to have been located
at one end of the structure. Possible storage pits were located
both inside and outside the houses. The houses appear to sur-
round a central open space but other than that do not seem to be
ordered in any fashion. Kenyon believes that one house (No. 6)
had undergone extensive rebuilding for some unknown reason.
One possibility could be its destruction by fire.

The location of the palisade, like that of the houses was
determined by the excavation of post-mould features in the
subsoil. As can be seen in Figure 2.3, a single-rowed palisade
enclosed the entire perimeter of the village. No evidence of a
gate was found. While the post-moulds outlining the house
structures ranged from 2.25 to 4.0 inches in diameter, those that
formed the palisade ranged from 2.25 to 9.0 inches in diameter.
Larger posts were certainly employed in the construction of
fortifications. A third pattern of post-moulds (not indicated on
Figure 2.3) also emerged from the excavations. The small posts
(1.25-2.5 inches in diameter) that produced these post-moulds
formed curved lines of irregular length to which no significance
has yet been attributed.

Recent excavations at the nearby Boys site, also an Early
Ontario Iroquois village, suggest that this settlement contained
houses similar in size and shape to those of the Miller site.[33] A
palisade, and this time a gate, are also in evidence. More
detailed observations must await the analysis of the past
season's excavations.

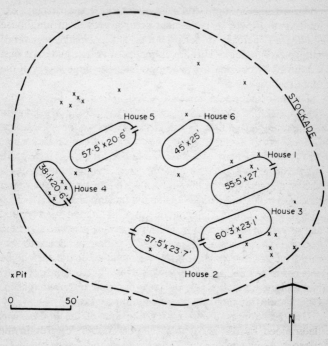

2.3   The Miller site, schematic floor plan. After Kenyon, 1968.

The village pattern of the Middle Ontario Iroquois stage is distinctly different. Although no settlements in the Toronto area, related to this time period, have seen the extensive excavation carried out at the Miller site, evidence in the form of an entire village floor plan is available for a Middle Ontario Iroquois village excavated near Port Elgin, Ontario.[34] The relatively small size of this village (approximately 2.75 acres compared to a mean of approximately 3.5 acres for the Toronto area villages) may be due to its isolated location and possible special function. Wright suggests that the inhabitants of this Nodwell site moved to the Lake Huron shore in order to establish trade relations with the Algonkian speaking bands of the Upper Great Lakes. Whatever the reason, we should not regard this village plan as typical of the Middle Ontario Iroquois stage. At the same

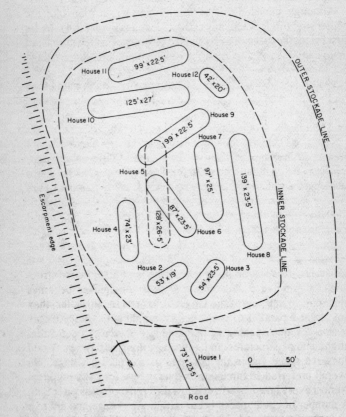

House 11 — 99' x 22.5'

House 12

House 12 — 42' x 20'

House 10 — 125' x 27'

House 9

House 5 — 99' x 22.5'

House 7

OUTER STOCKADE LINE

INNER STOCKADE LINE

House 6 — 87' x 23.5'

House 6 — 97' x 25'

House 8 — 139' x 23.5'

House 4 — 74' x 23'

128' x 26.5'

House 8

House 2 — 53' x 19'

House 3 — 54' x 23.5'

Escarpment edge

N

House 1 — 73' x 23.5'

0   50'

Road

2.4   The Nodwell site, schematic floor plan. After Wright, 1971.

time it probably exhibits some of the characteristics of a village site of this time period, and since it is the only site for which detailed settlement plans exist, it cannot be overlooked.

Although the Nodwell village is circular in plan like the Miller site, this is where any similarities end (Figure 2.4). In the first place, the palisade is composed of two rows of posts that are up to sixty-five feet apart on the eastern boundary of the village but then almost merge adjacent to the ravine on the western boundary. There is evidence that stone tool manufacturing took place in the area between the two stockades. Palisade posts, as evidenced by the post-moulds in the subsoil, were between 5 and 12 inches in diameter.[35]

The size, spacing and orientation of houses exhibits even greater differences between the Early and Middle Ontario Iroquois stages. Although three of the Nodwell houses are of a size and shape similar to Miller site structures, the remainder of the twelve longhouses excavated are certainly more substantial. The longest of these measured 139 feet in length while still maintaining a width of 23.5 feet (Figure 2.4). The widths of all of the longhouses are in fact between nineteen and twenty-seven feet and as such do not differ significantly from the Miller site structures. In addition to an increasing length for house structures, a semblance of ordering for the longhouses becomes apparent. In the case of the longer structures in particular, they are aligned parallel to their nearest neighbour. One possible reason for this spacing is immediately obvious: the parallel alignment of structures and especially long structures would conserve space within the confines of so small a village. No overall preferred alignment, however, exists for the structures. Almost every house is oriented to a different compass direction. A number of open spaces occur within the village and are to a large degree surrounded by house structures. These are located between houses 6 and 8 in the southern portion of the village, between houses 7 and 9 in the centre of the village and between houses 12 and 8 in the northeastern portion of the village. A large open area also extends from house 9 to the western extremity of the palisade. The function, if any, of these spaces remains open to question. Mr. A. Tyyska, an archaeologist with the Historical Sites Branch of the Ministry of Natural Resources for Ontario, feels that the inhabitants of the longhouses surrounding each open area in a Huron village may have belonged to the same lineage or clan.[36] If this can also be attributed to the Huron's Middle Ontario Iroquois ancestors, a number of lineages may have occupied the Nodwell village. This does not seem to be in evidence for the Miller site.

The location of house 1 outside the stockade may appear odd at first glance. Wright suggests that this structure was probably erected prior to the main population influx. It may in fact have been constructed at the same time as house 5 which was later destroyed or taken down and replaced by houses 6 and 9. The pinched stockade near the northern extremity of house 1 tends to support the theory that this house was constructed before the stockade.

The longhouses at Nodwell contained in excess of sixteen hundred pits dug by the inhabitants. These pits held everything from food to ceremonial burials as is evidenced by the excavated remains. This profusion of pits covered the interiors of the houses (not shown in Figure 2.4) and was certainly denser than the pit distribution reported for the Miller site. This may indicate that more was stored by the Nodwell inhabitants and on the other hand it may indicate that the Nodwell site saw a longer period of occupation. Both of these possibilities suggest development from the Early to the Middle Ontario Iroquois stage.

The development of the Ontario Iroquois village pattern appears to have culminated during the time period between 1400 and 1600 A.D. and then remained largely the same until the French suggested some changes to the Huron in 1636.[37] This resulted in the construction of a square village palisade and corner bastions at Ossossane. Although considerable information on village morphology for the Late Ontario Iroquois period is still required before any conclusive statements can be made about the stabilization of the village pattern, the settlement pattern information presently available for both the prehistorical and historical time periods suggests few substantial changes in village morphology.

Again, the Late Ontario Iroquois sites of the Toronto area have seen relatively little excavation for settlement patterns. This situation is presently changing with the initiation of an ambitious project, financed by the Federal Ministry of Transport, to excavate the entire ten acres of the Draper site to be destroyed upon construction of the proposed Pickering Airport. In fact, two longhouse structures and portions of a third and fourth have already been uncovered at Draper.[38] Longhouse structures also have been excavated at the MacLeod site in Oshawa[39] and at the McKenzie and Parsons sites in the Toronto area.[40] Portions of palisade structures have also been uncovered at all of these sites. The settlement patterns for all of the sites appear to be similar. Since none of these villages has to date seen a complete excavation, no conclusive remarks can be formulated. The evidence, however, does indicate that all of the villages, except the MacLeod site, were enclosed by palisades. In the case of the MacLeod site, a palisade may have existed but is undetected because the site was only partially excavated. The site also may be of the dispersed village type described by Heidenreich for Huronia.[41] In this case the village consisted of a number of longhouses, with no apparent plan, located along a watercourse.

All of the villages, including the MacLeod site, contained longhouses of substantial length. A completely excavated house at the McKenzie site measured 174 feet by 28 feet.[42] The houses uncovered at Draper were both in excess of 150 feet in length. The MacLeod site structures are both in excess of 100 feet in length.[43] No short structures have been located on any of these sites.

The settlement patterns of these villages exhibit continuity in another respect. All of the house structures are aligned roughly in a northwest to southeast direction and parallel to each other within the villages. One likely reason for this, as mentioned previously, might be the conservation of space. Another reason has recently been suggested. Norcliffe and Heidenreich[44] claim that the northwest to southeast alignment, which exposes the least amount of longhouse surface to prevailing winds, may have been an attempt by the Ontario Iroquois to maximize thermal efficiency. One might well expect that the longhouse would be an extremely cold place in which to live if its broad side continually faced the prevailing winds. A greater amount of surface area to the wind might also heighten the danger of the post-supported, bark structure being levelled in a storm.

The Huron villages of historical times were much like their

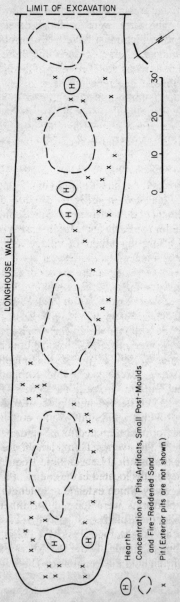

2.5 The Draper site, schematic floor plan. Courtesy B. Hayden and Ontario Archaeological Society.

LIMIT OF EXCAVATION

LONGHOUSE WALL

0   10   20   30'

H Hearth

⌀ Concentration of Pits, Artifacts, Small Post-Moulds
     and Fire-Reddened Sand

× Pit (Exterior pits are not shown)

predecessors of the prehistorical portion of the Late Ontario Iroquois stage. The sites were in most cases fortified by palisades, some of which must have been formidable indeed. Palisades at Cahiague, a large double village site near Orillia, were composed of as many as seven rows of posts.[45] A possible seven-rowed palisade has recently been discovered for the Draper site in the Toronto area. In addition to similarities in fortification, the Huron settlements exhibited characteristics of longhouse spacing and alignment much like those of the Late Ontario Iroquois villages. Houses were grouped parallel to each other and often aligned in a northwest to southeast direction.[46]

Although no Late Ontario Iroquois settlements have been completely excavated, a number of individual longhouses have been carefully excavated in order to provide details of the internal arrangement of these structures. Since comparative data are not available for the Early and Middle stages of the Ontario Iroquois, I will afford this aspect of village morphology only brief treatment. The recent excavations at the Draper site have exposed a house 28 feet wide and in excess of 150 feet in length (Figure 2.5). In addition to the numerous pits located in the house, there are central hearth features, spaced along the axis of the structure and clusters of small posts located near the hearths. The location of the artifacts within the longhouse suggest an adze manufacturing area and a smoking pipe use or manufacturing area. The morphology of the Huron longhouse is very similar. A structure, excavated at the Robitaille site near Penetanguishene, Ontario, provides the same evidence of central hearths, pits and clusters of small posts near the hearths.[47]

Heidenreich provides a summary of the archaeological and ethnohistorical information related to the interior arrangement of the longhouse.[48] The average Huron longhouse (and this can also apply to the prehistorical Late Ontario Iroquois longhouse) had three to four hearths located in the centre of a ten to twelve foot wide passageway which extended the length of the structure. Sleeping platforms were located on either side of the passageway. Under these platforms, as well as at the ends of the houses, were located the storage areas. Two families made use of every hearth but also made use of numerous smaller fires that were scattered throughout the longhouse. These were probably the cooking fires.

The village pattern, and also the longhouse pattern, of the Historic Huron appears to be the culmination of a development in village and dwelling morphology that began about 900 A.D. and achieved its final form between 1500 and 1600 A.D. Village and longhouse patterns were then perpetuated into the historical period. Although a great deal of settlement pattern analysis is still required to support these observations, the development of the Ontario Iroquois is well documented on other grounds. These include the development of their material culture, their agriculture and their social organization.[49] That their village patterns also developed, should logically follow. Our present lack of knowledge about this process is understandable for the excavation of an entire village is an extremely formidable and time-consuming task. But only through such excavations can the process of settlement pattern development be documented.

Prehistorical and Historical Settlement in the Toronto Area

A first glance at the distribution of prehistorical villages illustrated in Figure 2.1 may well convey an impression of a lack of order. This has hopefully been abated by the previous discussions on village distribution and site characteristics. There certainly was a different landscape organization between the prehistorical and the historical settlement. While the prehistorical settlement distribution and site location were guided mainly by decisions that were based upon a thorough knowledge of the environment, the historical settlement distribution and site location of European peoples were governed by numerous controls among which the survey system stands out.[50] Although both types of settlement required a reliable water source, the type of source employed by the historical agricultural village was more likely a stream or river than a spring. Not only would one expect very few springs to coincide with the grid of the survey system but one would also expect the historical village in a location where it could exploit the potential power of water as well.[51] One can go on to point out quite obvious differences in the distribution and site characteristics of the two types of settlement. It suffices to say that the differences are explained by reference to the two basically different ways of life which in turn are the function of differences in economy, technology and social structure.

These differences in economy, technology and social structure are also brought out in the settlement pattern. Unlike the palisaded agglomeration of longhouses that constituted the Ontario Iroquois village, the historical village, structured by the survey system and protected by the crown, consisted of a few buildings differentiated by function and often clustered about transportation and industrial facilities. Differences in technology and social structure are especially important in explaining the differences between the longhouse and the relatively substantial house structure erected by the early settler. While the prehistorical villagers had only crude tools at their disposal, the historical settler could draw upon not only the relatively advanced tools he brought along, but also on the accumulated knowledge of hundreds of intervening years of technological development. A difference in technology can explain the choice and utilization of building materials but a basic difference in social structure explains the variation in form.[52] While the Ontario Iroquois longhouse was constructed to house a number of nuclear families all belonging to the same extended family, the historical settler's home was constructed for the nuclear family only. As a result of all these differences, the angular and uniform, log or frame structures of the historical settlement stand in sharp contrast to the elongated, ovate and dishevelled appearance of the Ontario Iroquois longhouse.

The foregoing discussion provides only a brief and superficial overview of the basic differences in the distribution, site and pattern of prehistorical and historical settlements. In order to develop this theme and to relate it more specifically to the Toronto area, a considerable amount of additional research is required. This does not lie within the compass of this paper.

In the beleaguered search for evidence on the prehistorical settlement we may be fighting a losing battle against the spread of one of North America's fastest growing cities. New data retrieval techniques and a growing interest in prehistory are aiding the search, but before we have a chance to retrieve the knowledge the prehistorical sites may disappear.

Acknowledgements.

Thanks to J. V. Wright and W. A. Kenyon (and Royal Ontario Museum) each for permitting use of a diagram.

Notes

[1]A recent inventory of archaeological sites in Huronia has been compiled by Mr. Frank Ridley: *Huronia Survey,* Reports to the Ontario Department of Public Records and Archives (Toronto, 1966-1971).

[2]The Grand River valley has seen numerous archaeological surveys. A selection follows: G. F. MacDonald, "Archaeological Survey of the Grand River between Paris and Waterloo, Ontario, 1961," National Museums of Canada, Ottawa, n.d. W. J. Wintemberg, "Indian Village Sites in Oxford and Waterloo", *Annual Archaeological Report to the Minister of Education for Ontario,* 1900, pp. 83-92.

[3]Numerous surveys have also been conducted in southwestern Ontario. T.E. Lee, "A Preliminary Report on an Archaeological Survey of Southwestern Ontario in 1950", *National Museums of Canada Bulletin,* No. 126 (1950), pp. 64-75. W. C. Noble, "Report on Archaeological Field Studies and Sequences in Southwestern Ontario", on file with the Historical Sites Branch, Ontario Ministry of Natural Resources, 1971. D. Stothers, "The Archaeological Culture History of Southwestern Ontario", unpublished paper, Department of Sociology and Anthropology, University of Toledo, Ohio, 1972.

[4]C. E. Heidenreich, *Huronia/A History and Geography of the Huron Indians, 1600-1650* (Toronto: McClelland and Stewart, 1971).

[5]V. A. Konrad, *The Archaeological Resources of the Metropolitan Toronto Planning Area: Inventory and Prospect,* York University, Department of Geography Discussion Paper No. 10, 1973. The Archaeological Survey of the Metropolitan Toronto Area was supported in 1971 by the Secretary of State for Canada and in 1972 by the Archaeological Survey of Canada, National Museum of Man and the Royal Ontario Museum.

[6]J. V. Wright, *Ontario Prehistory* (Ottawa: Archaeological Survey of Canada, National Museum of Man, National Museums of Canada, 1972), p. 27.

[7]This dart head or "fluted point" was found near Markham during the 1930s. National Museum of Man, Cat. No. VII-F-23461.

[8]Wright, *Ontario Prehistory, op. cit.,* p. 11.

[9]B. G. Trigger, "The Destruction of Huronia: A Study in Economic

and Cultural Change, 1609-1650'', *Transactions of the Royal Canadian Institute*, No. 68, Vol. 33 (October 1960), pp. 14-45.

[10]Both of these villages appear on a number of early French maps of the area. The best locations are given on the following map. Public Archives of Canada, National Map Collection (Map No. H3-902): P. Raffeix, *Le Lac Ontario Avec Les Lieux Circonvoisins et Particulièrement Les Cinq Nations Iroquoises,* 1688. A history of Toronto during the early historical period is documented in: P. Robinson, *Toronto During the French Regime, 1615-1793* (Toronto: University of Toronto Press, 1965).

[11]Ontario, *16th Report of the Bureau of Archives of Ontario,* G. C. Paterson ''Land Settlement in Upper Canada, 1783-1840'' (Toronto, 1921), Chapter X, ''Indian Lands'', pp. 219-235.

[12]J. V. Wright, ''The Ontario Iroquois Tradition'', *National Museum of Canada Bulletin*, No. 210, 1966.

[13]The *''in situ''* theory is based upon ceramic evidence from sites in southern Ontario. R. S. MacNeish, ''Iroquois Pottery Types'', *National Museum of Canada Bulletin,* No. 124, 1952.

[14]Wright, ''Ontario Iroquois Tradition,'' *op. cit.* p. 54.

[15]J. N. Emerson, ''Problems of Huron Origins'', *Anthropologica,* Vol. 3, no. 2 (1961).

[16]Newcomb employs, among others, the technique of nearest neighbour analysis. He deals with Iron Age settlements, distinctive types of settlement within a distinctive prehistorical time period. These controls are not yet possible in Ontario prehistory. R. M. Newcomb, ''Geographical Location Analysis and Iron Age Settlement in West Penwith'', *Cornish Archaeology,* No. 7 (1968), pp. 5-14; *idem*, ''The Spatial Distribution Pattern of Hill Forts in West Penwith'', *Cornish Archaeology,* No. 9 (1970), pp. 47-52.

[17]Three separate aspects of settlement can be distinguished for the convenience of analysis. These are the *site*—the relationship between a settlement and the immediate physical environment; *pattern*—the relationship of one dwelling to another, sometimes irrespective of site; and *distribution*—the much wider aspects of settlement. E. Jones, *Human Geography* (New York: Praeger, 1966), pp. 114-115. Although all three aspects are treated in this paper, the data require an emphasis on site and pattern.

[18]S. de Champlain, *The Works of Samuel de Champlain*, 6 volumes, (H.P. Biggar, ed.) (Toronto: The Champlain Society, 1922-1936), pp. 124-125.

[19]Heidenreich, *Huronia, op.cit.,* p. 213.

[20]G. Sagard, *The Long Journey to the Country of the Hurons* [1632] (G.M. Wrong, ed.) (Toronto: The Champlain Society, 1939), pp. 92-93.

[21]Heidenreich, *Huronia, op. cit.*, pp. 213-216.

[22]C. E. Heidenreich, "The Natural Environment of Huronia and Huron Seasonal Activities", *Marburger Geographische Schriften*, Heft 50 (Marburg/Lahn, 1971), p. 107.

[23]A total of 35 separate survey accounts were consulted for this information. The manuscripts are on file with the Ontario Department of Lands and Forests and cover the years 1793 through 1829. For a complete listing see the bibliography in Konrad, *Archaeological Resources of the Metropolitan Toronto Planning Area*, pp. 158-60.

[24]The references to the Huron in this and the next four paragraphs are based on Heidenreich, "The Natural Environment of Huronia", *op. cit.*, pp. 107-109.

[25]The formula for determining the index of preference for a phenomenon is expressed as follows:

Index of Preference for Phenomenon X

$$= \frac{\% \text{ of Sites on Phenomenon X}}{\% \text{ of Phenomenon X in Total Area}}$$

[26]Heidenreich, "The Natural Environment of Huronia", *op. cit.*, p. 107.

[27]Konrad, *Archaeological Resources*, op. cit., p. 67.

[28]*Ibid.*, pp. 64-5, 69.

[29]W. C. Galinet, "The Evolution of Corn and Culture in North America", in S. Struever (ed.), *Prehistoric Agriculture* (New York: The Natural History Press, 1971), pp. 534-43.

[30]Wright, *Ontario Prehistory*, op. cit., p. 67.

[31]W. A. Kenyon, "A Late Woodland Site Near Pickering", in "New Pages of Prehistory, 1958," *Ontario History*, LI, No. 1 (1959) pp. 58-9; *idem*, "The Miller Site—1959," in "New Pages of Prehistory, 1959", *Ontario History*, LII, No. 1 (1960); *idem*, "The Miller Site," Ph.D. Dissertation, University of Toronto, 1967; *idem*, *The Miller Site*, Royal Ontario Museum, Art and Archaeology, Occasional Paper, No. 14, 1968.

[32]The discussion of the Miller Site village morphology is based on Kenyon (1968), *The Miller Site*, pp. 17-21.

[33]C.S. Reid, personal communication, August, 1973.

[34]The discussion of the Nodwell Site village morphology is based on J. V. Wright, "The Nodwell Site: A Mid-14th Century Iroquois Village", *Canadian Archaeological Association Bulletin*, No. 3 (1971), pp. 1-11.

[35]Personal observation, July, 1972.

[36]Refer to Heidenreich, *Huronia, op. cit.*, p. 145.

[37]R. G. Thwaites (ed.), *The Jesuit Relations and Allied Documents*

. . . *in New France, 1610-1791* (New York: Pageant Book Company, 1959), Volume 10, p. 53.

[38]These structures were excavated during the 1972 and 1973 field seasons by Ontario Archaeological Society field crews under the direction of Mrs. M. Latta and subsequently Mr. B. Hayden. Progress reports are on file with the Archaeological Survey of Canada, National Museums of Canada, Ottawa.

[39]M. Latta, "The MacLeod Site", Report to the Archaeological Survey of Canada, National Museums of Canada, 1973.

[40]These sites were excavated under the direction of Professor J. N. Emerson, Department of Anthropology, University of Toronto. Refer to Wright, *Ontario Iroquois Tradition*, pp. 69-72, for further information.

[41]Heidenreich, *Huronia, op. cit.*, pp. 145-146.

[42]Wright, *Ontario Iroquois Tradition, op. cit.*, p. 70.

[43]Latta, "MacLeod Site", pp. 11-12.

[44]G. B. Norcliffe and C. E. Heidenreich, "The Preferred Orientation of Iroquoian Longhouses in Ontario", unpublished manuscript, Department of Geography, York University, 1973.

[45]Heidenreich, *Huronia, op. cit.*, p. 140.

[46]*Ibid.* pp. 143-146.

[47]A. E. Tyyska, Notes on the Excavation of the Robitaille Site. Unpublished Manuscript, Department of Anthropology, University of Toronto, 1969.

[48]Heidenreich, *Huronia, op. cit.*, pp. 116-120.

[49]Wright, *Ontario Prehistory*, pp. 64-78; *Idem, Ontario Iroquois Tradition*, pp. 94-101.

[50]G. M. Craig, *Upper Canada—The Formative Years* (Toronto: McClelland and Stewart, 1963), pp. 20-41.

[51]R. L. Gentilcore, "The Beginnings of Settlement in the Niagara Peninsula (1782-1792)", *The Canadian Geographer*, VII (1963), p. 78.

[52]The role of technology as a modifying factor and social structure as a determinant of house form is summarized in the following work. A. Rapoport, *House Form and Culture* (Englewood Cliffs, N.J.: Prentice-Hall, 1969), Chapters 3 and 5.

3. A MILITARY COLONY IN A WILDERNESS: THE UPPER CANADA FRONTIER*

R. Louis Gentilcore and David Wood

The settlement geography of British North America was set on a new course by the revolt of the American Colonies. In the wake of the conflict, British territory had to provide a haven for American Loyalist refugees. Three areas were available. Nova Scotia (which included New Brunswick until 1784) was the most accessible and had the longest experience with British settlement; it received by far the majority of the Loyalists. Only a token number went to what was to become Lower Canada (in 1791), but they constituted the first immigration of an English-speaking group to the former French colony. West of Montreal, in what was to become Upper Canada, practically no white settlement had taken place. That territory awaited only alienation from Indian claims to expedite two British quests: land for the Loyalists, and a military base flanking the United States on the northwest. Ultimately Nova Scotia and New Brunswick received about 30,000 Loyalists, and Lower Canada about 7,000. If one can rely on the figure for land granted to Loyalists (nearly three million acres) in Durham's 1839 report, then it seems likely that Upper Canada received roughly 9,000 such refugees by the end of the 1780s, not counting the loyal Six Nations Indians.[1]

Settlement by Design

Early settlement in Ontario was directed by military authorities. The first occupied places were military posts from which the taking up of land was organized, as the Crown sought to build a viable, defensible community. The British design was given concrete expression by its first Lieutenant Governor, John Graves Simcoe. The observant La Rochefoucault-Liancourt said of him, in 1795,

> He is acquainted with the military history of all countries; no hillock catches his eye without exciting in his mind the idea of a fort, which might be constructed on the spot. . . .[2]

and Simcoe, explaining something of his intentions in 1793, said

> . . . for every purpose of Civilization, command of the Indians, and general Defence . . . on the Confluence of the main Branches of the Thames the Capital of Upper Canada, as soon as possible, ought to be Situated. But . . . it is not my intention at present to establish myself upon the Forks of the River Thames. . . . I shall content myself with rendering the Road between Burlington Bay and the River Thames . . . sufficiently commodious as a military Communication . . .
> . . . as . . . the safety of this Province should not depend upon so feeble a Barrier as (comparatively) the contemptible Fortress of Niagara, it is with great pleasure that I offer to you some Observations upon the Military Strength and naval Conveniency of Toronto (now York) which I propose immediately to occupy.[3]

The first component in Simcoe's plan was military movement. Two primary roads were planned (Figure 3.1). Dundas Street would run from Lake Ontario to the site of the future provincial capital at the head of navigation on the Thames River, a place safe from attack yet affording ready access to Lake Erie and border points to the south. The road would facilitate movement into the interior and help consolidate control over this part of the province. Yonge Street, north from Lake Ontario, was conceived as a military route to provide rapid communication with the upper lakes. A second component of the plan was a set of nucleated settlements, to be planted at intervals along the roads, at road and water junctions.

The Simcoe plan is incorporated in one of the earliest printed maps of Ontario (Figure 3.2). The map, accurately depicting provincial districts, counties, townships, main villages, towns

3.1   Sketch of Upper Canada by (Mrs.) Elizabeth P. Simcoe, which accompanied Lt. Gov. Simcoe's despatch No. 19, 19th October 1793. The forts and some settlements—Kingston, York and Queenstown—were in existence. Courtesy National Map Collection, Public Archives of Canada.

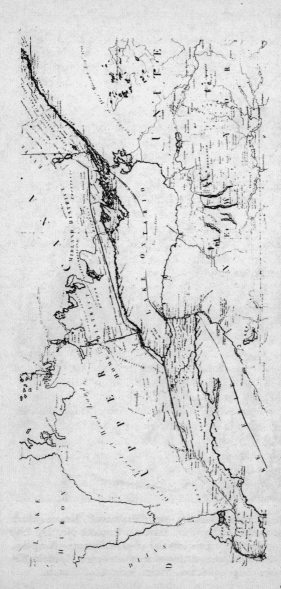

3.2 A portion of D.W. Smyth's 'A Map of the Province of Upper Canada, describing all the New Settlements, Townships, etc, with the Countries Adjacent, from Quebec to Lake Huron . . . 1800'. Courtesy Royal Ontario Museum, Toronto (957-185-1).

and Indian settlements, also includes roads and towns proposed by Simcoe but not in existence in 1800. For example, at this time there was no London, or Oxford (later Woodstock), nor a Dundas Street extending to them (although it had been surveyed). But many places which later became important urban centres were conceived as part of the plan. Toronto, the provincial capital, was the outstanding example. The plan also provided the impetus for places like Newmarket, Barrie, Penetanguishene, Woodstock, London and Chatham. One of its achievements was that it helped to direct population inland at a time when most of it still clung tenaciously to navigable waterways.

An operational analysis of the plan by Kirk, shortly after World War II, provided military terminology fitting to Simcoe's intentions. Kirk, extrapolating from Simcoe's correspondence, outlined the tactical advantages of the various nodal points in the resulting network and identified "bridgeheads" at the extremities of the military roads adjacent to the United States border (summarized in Figure 3.3).[4]

Setting and settlement

Combining with the Crown's efforts to direct settlement was a physical geography that both hindered and aided occupation and development. Most dominant was the forest, sensed, feared and appreciated in varying degrees as settlement advanced; so overpowering that new settlers had to be given detailed instructions on what to do for survival when lost in the woods. Not the least oppressive element in the partially-cleared countryside was the multitude of insects which afflicted both man and his beasts. W. H. Smith, in a wry aside in his *Gazetteer,* says

. . . mosquitoes are apt to form an early and sometimes rather *too intimate* an acquaintance with the newly arrived emigrant.[5]

The forest was both enemy and friend, an obstacle to be removed but also an asset, a source of food, building material and forage. It was in the woods that agriculture began. Land was cleared most commonly by cutting and burning, which might

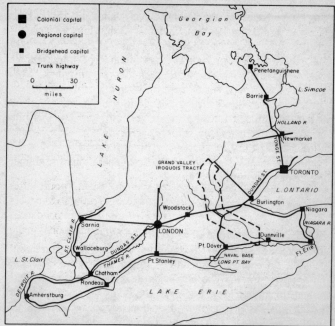

3.3 Kirk's 1949 summary of Simcoe's plan, southwestern Upper Canada.

require from a settler one month or more of hard labour per acre. Even then stumps were left standing, a reminder that the toil of clearing was not yet complete.[6] Fortunately, the task was not without early benefit. Clearing produced the settlers' first "cash crop". Ashes from the burned trees were preserved and sold to potash manufacturers. In some cases, especially where the settler had partially processed the ash himself, the "crop" might yield enough to pay the costs of clearing and fencing the land.[7]

The woods also contained the beginnings of Ontario's road network. Despite the Simcoe plan of trunk roads and the setting aside of road allowances as part of the land survey, much of the basic network before 1825 grew from Indian paths through the forest. For example, rivalling Dundas Street as a main east-west route was the Iroquois Trail, crossing the Niagara Peninsula at the foot of the escarpment and continuing westward. Adrian Marlet, surveying north of "The Governor's Road" (Dundas

Street) just east of the Grand River valley in 1816, noted
(Concession II, lot 19) "At 19 chains X old Mohawk Road", a
north-south route.[8] Along the north shore of Lake Ontario, the
Lakeshore Trail vied with Dundas Street. The importance of
water-side routes is obvious. Lakes and rivers provided the best
means of transport; roads were only supplements. As long as
settlement was thinly strung out along water routes, the road
pattern developed little beyond a series of spontaneous links
between the clusters of settlers, ignoring the gridiron road
allowances.[9] (The extension and improvement of roads as a
communication system during the first generation of settlement
are dealt with by McIlwraith, *infra*).

Agricultural beginnings

Slowly, the high roof of leaves was broken. But given the
abundance of land and the small population, agriculture could
only be an extensive operation. Implements were crude and
cultivation simple. The emphasis was on grains, particularly
wheat. In some places, however, the first food was Indian corn
which was easier to grow and produced more food, more reli-
ably on new land. But, in less than a decade, wheat was the
leading crop in all the settlements.[10] In the same period, wheat
also became a cash crop. As early as 1795, the fort at Kingston
was collecting wheat, together with peas and salt pork, for
export. If pioneering is to be equated with subsistence agriculture, its presence in early Ontario is very short-lived. From the
impetus provided by the fort settlements, commercial agriculture, based on wheat production, expanded into the nineteenth
century (*cf* Osborne on Kingston, *infra*). Indeed, wheat growing
quickly dominated or replaced what one might expect to be
persistent traditional crops, such as potatoes among Irish and
oats among Scots. The wooded landscape was replaced by open
stretches of cultivated fields, though commonly, in the opinion
of a priggish visitor, "ill-ploughed, . . . disfiguring the face of
the country" where "Corn succeeds corn, until the land is
nearly exhausted".[11] Increasing familiarity with the conditions
leading to farming success resulted in demand for better lands
and particularly those adjacent to the roads to main markets. It is
reported that although La Rochefoucault-Liancourt in 1795 had

thought Toronto to be a small swampy break in the woods (containing a fort and twelve log huts), by the mid-1840s "the three great thoroughfares—the western, the northern, and the Kingston roads—are each planked or macadamised for about twenty miles [out from Toronto]; and for the same distance nearly every lot fronting on the roads is taken up, settled, and under cultivation".[12]

The clearing of the woods also provided another major commodity for trade. The value of timber exports exceeded that of all agricultural products shipped from the province in the second quarter of the nineteenth century. The trade had been promoted by British policy dating back to the Napoleonic Wars.[13] Timber ships returning empty to North America offered the cheap link to complete the emigration chain. This symbiotic relationship sometimes was continued into Upper Canada through the demand of the timber camps for provisions and winter laborers. The most vigorous timber exploitation developed on the Ottawa River early in the nineteenth century, tapping many areas better suited to lumbering than to agriculture. Further southwest, the Trent River, on the edge of the Shield, also moved sizeable quantities of timber. Elsewhere, smaller scale exploitations were associated with numerous minor rivers and creeks throughout the province. (See Head's paper on forest exploitation in this volume).

The Port and Administration Functions

The increasing importance of exports fortified the early and persistent relationship between populated places and water, illustrated on the map of "populated places" in 1825 (Fig 3.4). The map also emphasizes the role of ports as entry points. Only three places, all ports, had populations of at least 1,000: Kingston the leading port; York, later Toronto, the capital; and Niagara, the original capital. Each occupied a key site in Simcoe's settlement plan; each was nurtured by a major fort from which settlement was deployed to nearby hinterlands and to which produce and equipment moved for handling and shipment. Between 1825 and 1851, the province's population increased from 158,000 to 952,000 (which surpassed that of the former Lower Canada). In 1806 it had been 71,000, compared

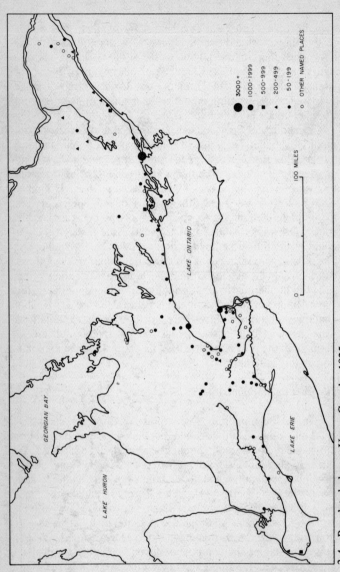

3.4 Populated places, Upper Canada, 1825.

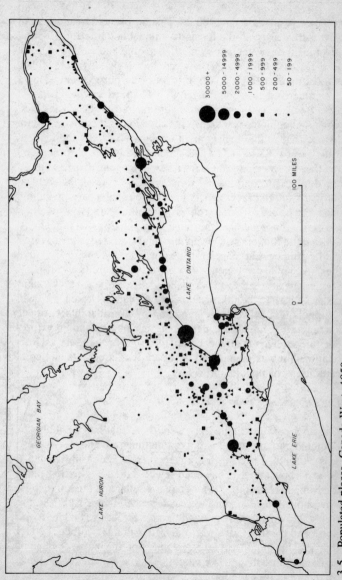

●	30000 +
●	5000 - 14999
●	2000 - 4999
●	1000 - 1999
■	500 - 999
■	200 - 499
◄	50 - 199

GEORGIAN BAY

LAKE HURON

LAKE ONTARIO

LAKE ERIE

0   100 MILES

3.5 Populated places, Canada West, 1850.

to Lower Canada's 250,000. Populated places advanced in a wave across parts of the formerly uninhabited interior. But the attachment to water survived, tied to the increased trade in timber, flour and wheat. There were now eighteen places with a population exceeding 2,000; thirteen were ports (Figure 3.5).

Another function contributed to growth. From the inception of settlement, centres awarded administrative responsibilities possessed unique advantages. The division of the province into districts led to the management of local affairs by the district court from 1788 to 1841. The appointed Justices of the Peace, meeting as The Court of Quarter Sessions in the district centre, not only tried court cases; they supervised road and bridge construction contracts and issued various licences, including those for taverns.[14] Their duties were adminstrative as well as judicial. Consequently, the places chosen for their meetings took on the role of district capitals. Once created, they became the leading central places for the areas around them. Initially, the choice of district centres was governed by military consider- ations and accessibility by water. As settlements grew, new districts had to be formed and new places chosen as their "capitals", a process accompanied by considerable political maneuvering (Ennals's paper, *infra*, on Cobourg and Port Hope documents a comparable competition). Throughout, a close relationship was maintained between district centres and con- centrations of population.

The Dominant Urban Nuclei

The dominant places in 1851 were those that had been able to combine port and administrative functions. The largest of these was Toronto. Offering the advantages of defensibility and a good harbour, the site had been selected for a key settlement in the Simcoe plan (Fig. 3.6). A naval arsenal and the provisional government headquarters were established there. By 1796, the original town lots were granted, Yonge Street was opened to the north and the first farms were emerging along it. Simcoe's view that the location was a logical one for the advancement of settlement into the interior would be borne out. But at the time, the community gave little indication of its future prominence. Even the Yonge Street artery was maintained irregularly and without conviction. York possessed only twelve cabins and a hinterland practically devoid of white population. There was no church, school or inn and only one store. In 1810 its population had risen to a modest 600, but the physical framework for growth had been established. The planted settlement continued to grow. By 1825, the population had more than doubled, to 1,677; at city incoroporation, in 1834, it was 9,252; in 1851 it stood at 30,775.[15] The city had held on to its function as the provincial capital, its port was a busy one, and its hinterland was no longer wilderness but productive and prosperous farmland, contributing wheat for export and drawing immigrants to its unsettled margins. Despite its prominence, Toronto differed little in appearance from other urban places in the province. It still struck visitors as a backwoods settlement. There were no paved streets; houses were small; the buildings were of wood, one storey high, except for a few three storey brick buildings in the main business area. The buildings sprawled along the blocks, including rows of sheds and huts, housing workers and the poor, in places betraying the outlines of incipient ghettoes.[16] There also were many examples of gaping vacant lots being held for speculation. But appearance masked the reality. By mid-century, Toronto dominated the urban geography of Ontario. It was the province's main wholesaling and distributing centre; banks and businesses, workshops and stores vied for space. In the early 1840s, building ground in the business area sold at the "incredible" rates of £10 to £20 a foot. The loss of its capital function for a few years in the 1840s and disastrous fires in 1847 and 1849 were only minor setbacks to Toronto's growth. The fires cleared away old buildings to make way for the new, a process that would become increasingly characteristic of the city as the rate of growth accelerated.

Second in size to Toronto in 1851, with about one-half its population (14,112) was the young city of Hamilton (Fig. 3.5) which is not even on the map of 1825. Like Toronto, Hamilton had begun as an administrative centre in the wilderness. Despite the claims of a number of thriving centres around it, the Hamilton townsite was chosen in 1816 as the centre for the new district of Gore. Later a port function was added in 1830 with the cutting of a channel through the bar that separated its potential harbour from Lake Ontario. By 1840, most of the grain produced in the

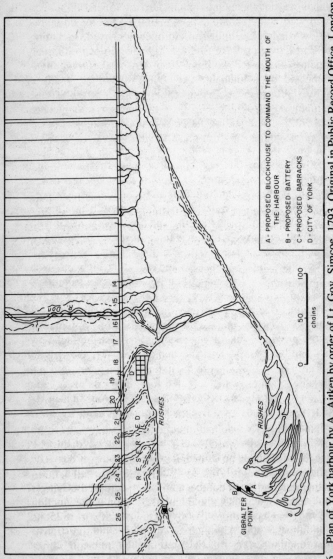

3.6 Plan of York harbour by A. Aitken by order of Lt. Gov. Simcoe, 1793. Original in Public Record Office, London. Redrawn from copy in the Toronto Public Library.

A - PROPOSED BLOCKHOUSE TO COMMAND THE MOUTH OF THE HARBOUR

B - PROPOSED BATTERY

C - PROPOSED BARRACKS

D - CITY OF YORK

farmlands west of Lake Ontario was moving to Hamilton. The city also vied with Toronto as a main entry point for immigration. New roads were built and old ones improved, including one to Port Dover on Lake Erie for the transport of iron mined and smelted on Long Point Bay. Other transportation improvements helped the settlement. The completion of the Welland Canal by 1830 provided a replacement for the Niagara portage as the main route from Lake Erie to Lake Ontario, and incidentally fulfilled a longstanding desire of colonial administrators to move the passage away from the United State boundary. Simcoe, in his correspondence (Vol. I, p. 90), misguidedly expressed the hope that a water route *via* the Upper Thames would "annihilate the political consequence of Niagara & Lake Erie." Hamilton used the canal, ironically, to import coal from Lake Erie ports in the United States, installing steam power facilities that would serve as a base for the expansion of industry. The ascendancy of Hamilton over other places in the area was typical of new urban growth in the province. Older settlements dependent upon intermittent water supplies for power and with limited shipping facilities, were declining in importance. Replacing them were urban centres on good harbours with easy access to new sources of power. In the Niagara Peninsula a new alignment of centres had been brought about by the construction of the Welland Canal (compare Fig. 3.4 & 3.5). Settlements on the Niagara River, including Niagara, the former capital, were now eclipsed by those on the canal, particularly St. Catharines, the terminus on Lake Ontario.

Ontario's third city in 1851 had been its leading one before 1825. Kingston grew up around the major fort built to guard entry into eastern Ontario and to organize its settlement. From the fort, a number of townships were surveyed for occupance by refugee loyalists from the United States in the early 1780s. The townsite was laid out in 1788. By 1800, there were half a dozen quays in operation. Their number and extent increased as Kingston took advantage of its harbour and its location at the junction of lake and river navigation. The town grew rapidly; in 1825, its population was 3,000. Although maintaining its administrative and port functions, it steadily lost ground to Toronto and Hamilton as trade was diverted from the Lake Ontario-St. Lawrence route to the United States via the Erie Canal. In 1851 it had a population of 11,697. (Osborne's essay, later in this book, traces Kingston's rise and fall). Port cities above and below Kingston also were marked for decline (and even Montreal's "tradeshed" was truncated). But they were prominent in the urban geography of the province in 1825 and even in 1850 when they were still able to tap productive hinterlands.

Another settlement whose fortunes were tied to water was Bytown, Ontario's fourth largest in 1851. The Bytown location had developed as a centre for the lumber trade, beginning with the floating of squared white pine logs down the Ottawa River to Quebec; in the late 1830s and through the 1840s the watershed was the largest producer of timber in North America. A second and more immediate impetus to growth was selection of the site as terminus and headquarters for the building of the Rideau Canal between the Ottawa River and Kingston. The town's population had reached 7,760 by 1851. Bytown was eventually made a district centre and later, rechristened "Ottawa", it began a new life on the strength of an administrative impetus *par excellence*.

The only sizeable inland city in 1851 was London, whose population of 7,035 made it the fifth largest in Ontario. Although the site had been chosen by Simcoe as the future provincial capital, there was no town or village there in 1825. But the crown had retained the proposed townsite and made it a district centre in 1826. Drawing sustenance from a well-settled hinterland and assisted by business generated from its administrative operations, London grew steadily, the pace quickening in the 1840s in response to increasing agricultural production.

Growth was not assured everywhere in the province even by the vital functions of port and administration. For example, Goderich on Lake Huron was planned as the administrative centre for the colonizing activities of the Canada Company in western Ontario. The settlement had a good harbour, served as the terminus of two main roads and was also a district centre. But the port was never active and no sizable population emerged. Goderich could not overcome the disadvantages of a peripheral situation. The area around it was sparsely populated and the main settled parts of the province were too far away. Similar difficulties confronted other western settlements, in-

cluding those along the Detroit River. Amherstburg was a
military settlement, at the junction of the Detroit River and Lake
Erie, which also failed to grow. By 1850 it was being overshadowed by the more favourably situated Windsor-Sandwich
area which would draw strength from its location across from
the city of Detroit and its role as a district centre.

Hindrances to growth in Upper canada were not merely
"situational". Nor are they encompassed within a broader
category including land quality, which would largely explain
the failure of settlement on the Laurentian Shield a generation
later. As identified by the impatient Robert Gourlay (1817ff)
and recognized by the famous report by Lord Durham (1839),
there were considerable social hindrances. Gourlay was concerned about privilege, which embraced the alienation of scattered lots of potential farmland granted to friends of government
and to Crown and Clergy. The quantity of such land is astonish-
ing. Durham's report calculates that, *omitting* Crown but including Clergy reserves, these grants amounted to nearly half
the 17,000,000 surveyed acres in the province! W.H. Smith's
Gazetteer (1846) shows the various kinds of grants in a table in
which the sums tend to be a little higher than Durham's. Smith's
table has an air of authenticity, but no source is given and it is
difficult to compare with the exhaustively-mined data presented
by Lillian Gates in her 1968 publication.[17] The wildness of
much of the reserved land irritated and inconvenienced bona
fide settlers all across the province. There are numerous examples of speculators who held thousands of acres widespread
throughout the province before the middle of the century.
"Privilege" also embraced a patronizing and aloof style of
governing, which dominated Upper Canada through the 1830s,
and which was blatantly at odds with the equality of opportunity
underlying the influential American Doctrine of Success.[18]

Conclusion

The pattern of urban development in mid-nineteenth century
Ontario cannot be divorced from the countryside in which it was
imbedded. The growth of market and service centres accompanied increasing wheat and timber production, particularly

after 1825. But those places in which growth was quickened
possessed certain advantages over their neighbours. Principal
among these were administrative and port functions, spawned in
some cases by a plan of development proposed for the province
when settlement was in its infancy. By 1850 the major urban
places had emerged. They retained the traditional association
with well established transportation routes. But more important
was the increasing concentration in a cluster around Toronto and
Hamilton, at the western end of Lake Ontario, the forerunner of
to-day's "Golden Horseshoe". In the decades that followed,
the province would move from a simple resource exploitation
economy, focussed on agriculture, toward a more industrial and
commercial one, ushered in by the coming of railways in the
1850s. But these developments would not change the urban
pattern. They would work within it, concentrating growing
populations in a limited number of places whose propensity for
growth had been indicated before 1850. This was the most
momentous of the legacies of John Graves Simcoe to Ontario.

Notes

*This paper is based, in part, on R. L. Gentilcore, "Ontario Emerges
from the Trees", *Geographical Magazine*, Vol. XLV, no. 5 (February,
1973), pp. 383-391 (by courtesy of *The Geographical Magazine*,
London).

[1] *cf* Gerald M. Craig, *Upper Canada/The Formative Years/
1784-1841* (Toronto: McClelland and Stewart, 1963), chapter 1.

[2] *La Rochefoucault-Liancourt's Travels in Canada, 1795 . . .* , edited
with notes by William R. Riddell, published as *Thirteenth Report of the
Bureau of Archives for the Province of Ontario . . . (1916)* (Toronto
1917), pp. 38-39.

[3] *The Correspondence of Lieut. Governor John Graves Simcoe, with
Allied Documents Relating to His Administration of the Government of
Upper Canada*, collected and edited by E.A. Cruikshank (Toronto:
Ontario Historical Society, 1923), Vol. I, pp. 338, 339 (31st May,
1793).

[4] Donald W. Kirk, "Southwestern Ontario/The Areal Pattern of
Urban Settlements in 1850", unpublished doctoral thesis, Northwest-
ern University, 1949, especially Figure 12, p. 56.

[5] W. H. Smith, *Smith's Canadian Gazetteer . . .* (Toronto: H. & W.

Rowsell, 1846), (reprinted in Coles Canadiana Collection), p. 241.

[6]Kenneth Kelly, "Wheat Farming in Simcoe County in the mid-Nineteenth Century", *The Canadian Geographer,* xv (1971), pp. 95-112, gives an extended description of the common stages of clearing. See also Kelly's essay in this volume.

[7]William Cattermole, *Emigration. The Advantages of Emigration to Canada* . . . (London: Simpkin and Marshall, 1831), (reprinted in Coles Canadiana Collection), pp. 85-86.

[8]Marlet's survey notebook of Dumfries township is on file at the Survey Records Office, Ontario Department of Natural Resources. The prime source on the survey books is R.L. Gentilcore and K. Donkin, *Land Surveys of Southern Ontario/An Introduction and Index to the Field Notebooks of the Ontario Land Surveyors/1784-1859,* Cartographica monograph No. 8, York University, B.V. Gutsell, 1973.

[9]Andrew Burghardt, "The Origin and Development of the Road Network of The Niagara Peninsula, Ontario, 1770-1851", *Annals,* Association of American Geographers, LIX (1969), pp. 417-440.

[10]R. L. Gentilcore, "The Beginnings of Settlement in the Niagara Peninsula (1782-1792)", *The Canadian Geographer,* VII (1963), pp. 72-82, and K. Kelly, "Wheat Farming in Simcoe County . . .", *The Canadian Geographer,* xv (1971), pp. 95-112.

[11]John Howison, *Sketches of Upper Canada, Domestic, Local, and Characteristic* . . . (Edinburgh: Oliver and Boyd, 1821), (reprinted in Coles Canadiana Collection) pp. 193, 146.

[12]W.H. Smith, *Smith's Canadian Gazetteer.* . . , 1846, p. 244.

[13]A.R.M. Lower, provides the classical analysis in "The Trade in Square Timber" (1933), reprinted in W.T. Easterbrook and M.H. Watkins (eds.), *Approaches to Canadian Economic History,* The Carleton Library No. 31 (1967), pp. 28-48.

[14]Frederick H. Armstrong, *Handbook of Upper Canadian Chronology and Territorial Legislation* (London, Ont.: University of Western Ontario, 1967), pp. 137, 149 *passim.*

[15]Peter G. Goheen, *Victorian Toronto, 1850 to 1900: Pattern and Process of Growth,* The University of Chicago, Department of Geography, Research Paper No. 127, 1970, p. 49. A standard source is Donald Kerr and Jacob Spelt, *The Changing Face of Toronto—A study in Urban Geography,* Memoir 11, Geographical Branch, Canada Dept. of Mines and Technical Surveys, Ottawa, 1965.

[16]F.H. Armstrong, "The Toronto Directories and the Negro Community in the late 1840s", *Ontario History,* LXI (1969), pp. 111-119.

[17]John George Lambton, Lord Durham, *The Report of the Earl of Durham* . . . , new edition (London: Methuen, 1902), pp. 155, 158. W.H. Smith, *Smith's Canadian Gazetteer* (Toronto, 1846), p. 242.

Lillian F. Gates, *Land Policies of Upper Canada,* Canadian Studies in History and Government No. 9 (University of Toronto Press, 1968), pp. 139, 140.

¹⁸Fred Landon, *Western Ontario and the American Frontier* [1941], The Carleton Library No. 34 (Toronto: McClelland and Stewart Ltd., 1967), Foreword, *passim.*

4. TRANSPORTATION IN THE LANDSCAPE OF EARLY UPPER CANADA

Thomas F. McIlwraith

The first half of the nineteenth century was marked by a flurry of innovation in transportation in North America. The canal, the plank road, and the railway have attracted the attention of scholars because they contributed to making inland areas, far from navigable waters, accessible at about the same time that such areas came to the attention of the expanding colonial seaboard populations.[1] The causal linkages between settlement and access are complex, but there is no doubt that all settlers in North America intended to engage in commerce, and innovations in transport apparently contributed to achieving this goal.

It is noteworthy, then, that there were inland areas which did progress from raw forest to refined, export-oriented, agricultural communities in the absence of such innovations. Upper Canada generally fits the mold. For that reason, this essay is focussed not upon modes but upon the use made of transportation among Upper Canada's settler-farmers—that is, to use the terminology of diffusion theory, upon the acceptor rather than the innovator.[2] On the farm, in the rural neighbourhood, and for commercial affairs in the wider world, settlers established what might reasonably be called a vernacular form: traditional procedures mixed with local expedients which together provided the necessary level of mobility.

On the Farm

The making and operating of farms engaged the attention of more than three-quarters of the population of Upper Canada in any year prior to the 1850s.[3] Such was the nature of land

51

disposal, with its reserves, patronage, and so forth, that settlement was characterized by dispersion first, later followed by filling up those vacant lots which surrounded the now-established farms of the first residents of the neighbourhood.[4] Thus, for more than half a century the mixture of farm contruction and farm operation prevailed over hundreds of square miles of southern Ontario. The daily round of felling trees, raising houses or barns, making fences, tending crops, cutting fuel-wood, and witnessing the painfully slow retreat of the edges of the clearing (probably no more than 100 feet per year in any one direction): here was the stuff of creating a commercial agricultural community, and the process called for countless short trips within the lot.

For the settler tackling a lot not more than ten years removed from a state of primeval forest, a large proportion of his time and energy was spent in farm-making. Transportation in his experience meant hauling: the best logs to be drawn from the spot where felled to the cabin site for building, poorer ones to be stacked somewhere else for cutting into firewood, and the worst and the slash to be drawn into piles for firing. Stumps and boulders had to be extracted, and cedar pulled out of the swampy spots for splitting into fence rails. All of this called for brute force. Simple dragging was far more appropriate than using wheeled wagons through the tangle of construction, provided sufficient power could be applied.

A team of oxen was a man's greatest asset during the farm-making years. ''A couple of oxen, a cow, two pigs, a harrow, and an axe'': these were the assets one writer recommended to a prospective settler in the 1820s.[5] Fitted with a shoulder yoke to which a chain was secured, oxen provided the slow, steady power that no horse could deliver, and certainly dwarfed the capabilities of men short of Paul Bunyan. Oxen were cheaper than horses to purchase, quicker to mature, hardier, and could be fattened for slaughter at the end of their working life. They performed with consistency through summer hard pan, spring mud, or winter snow. The advantages of reduced friction in winter were not pertinent in the farm-making situation, as ice reduced traction and froze into the ground logs to be moved. Heavy work in winter in the farm-making districts was popular for the same reasons that it was in lumber camps: namely, it complemented the farm production schedule and hot, sweaty work was most comfortable in cool temperatures, for man and beast alike.

A reasonable counting of the number of oxen per household is impossible because of overlapping census definitions and the fact that the ox of February could become the milk cow of July.[6] While circumstantial evidence strongly suggests that every household needed oxen, not all owned a team. Most families had access to one, however, and borrowing in exchange for labour or goods was a familiar procedure made possible by the fact that no one man could keep a yoke fully employed the year round.[7] It might be possible to estimate the number of households that could share the services of one team, but the question of sufficient numbers of oxen being available is only answerable in the vaguest fashion. All the interrelated topics of animal prices, reproduction rates, working life expectancy, and changing rates of farm-making are involved. One observer's surprise at a settler not using oxen in his clearing operation raises real doubts regarding their availability in sufficient numbers.[8]

In the Neighbourhood

Beyond the clearings lay the rural neighbourhood, a patch-work of woods and rough clearings in which the former was the decidedly predominant element through the first half of the nineteenth century.[9] A rectangular system of road allowances had been included in the original lot survey, and legislation existed for their opening, maintenance and improvement.[10] There are clear indications, however, that the result in the majority of cases would not be graced by the title "road" in our modern experience. One may visualize a countryside of wagon-width paths wandering from side to side within the sixty-six foot bounds of the right-of-way, bypassing a rock here and a stump there. This adherence to the surveyed limits was only a convenience, and there was no hesitation about deviating onto what was—or later became—private property, in order to avoid a swamp, hill, or other obstruction.[11]

In places where a road passed through clearings it must have been nearly indistinguishable from them—field and road alike were dotted with stumps, and neither fences nor ditches were

4.1 "View from the summit of the ridge above Nicholl's Tavern, Penetanguishene Road"; painting by Dartnell 1836. Courtesy Royal Ontario Museum, Toronto (952-87-8).

certainties in the early days. Elsewhere, as the road passed through woods, trees joined branches overhead and the thoroughfare proper became indistinguishable from the woods itself. The artist G.R. Dartnell has captured the essence of the road in Upper Canada in his watercolour, "On the Penetang Road" (1836),[12] in which the route passing the clearing in the foreground enters a black portal of trees in the background, totally disappearing. Roads most certainly were not the highly visible element in the landscape that they are today. (see Figure 4.1).

One might venture to say that the yoke of oxen had as much business on the roads as back in the clearings. This is indeed true, for road building and subsequent repairs. Oxen were also used for drawing logs to sawmills, or even to streams or the lakefront for export. In addition, oxen were needed on regularly-used roads during the wet seasons, spring and fall, to provide power for those who chose to be abroad at those times. Regarding Yonge Street, the main road north from Toronto, a commentator in 1846 remarked that "No farmer having any regard for his horses would allow them to travel on it".[13] Walking must not have been much of a pleasure either. Oxen may have deputized for horses, but to a large extent people simply arranged not to travel at muddy times, and certainly not to carry heavy loads. Oxen and horses alike stayed home.

Beyond the farm one encountered the domain of the pedestrian and the horse. The horse was prized for its speed and tractability rather than power. It is not to be imagined that horses were being galloped madly all over the place, and indeed quite a different image is presented by the poet Archibald Lampman in these lines:

> . . . slowly steals
> A hay-cart, moving dustily
>   With idly clacking wheels.
> At his cart's side the wagoner
>   Is slouching slowly at his ease,
> Half-hidden in the windless blur
>   Of white dust puffing to his knees.[14]

However, speeds double that of an ox team could be achieved by even the restrained use of horses, and even by walking. Furthermore, horses demonstrated that they could be used increasingly on the farm, while the oxen had a limited and diminishing role on the roads. The sensible farmer who saw the advantages of a dual-purpose animal relegated the oxen to the pasture they had helped to create.

Careful study of the few farm diaries surviving might give an actual measure of the frequency of expeditions off the farm, but circumstantial evidence may once again prove fully as revealing. One can imagine a family ten to fifteen years on the land, with children up to the teenage years, going to church most weeks, or making neighbourly social calls on many occasions, especially in winter or at times of lull in the farming activities. Individual family members might be called down the road to assist in a building project or the harvest, to attend a sick neighbour in the next farm, undertake the occasional ''shopping trip'' for tools, cloth, or salt, or simply check for mail at the post office. Children hiked a mile or more to school, where such was available. All of these purposes suggest a weekly average of three or four short expeditions by one or more members of the family. There were fewer trips for those more recently arrived in the neighbourhood, and a higher proportion of these were made by foot. A riding horse gave signs of coming up in the world, and those who held horses and carriages paid a tax for the luxury of riding splendidly (although rarely in comfort) through the countryside.[15]

Along the road in front passed an assortment of itinerant and occasional users. There was the pot-mender and boot maker, or possibly a doctor or clergyman on horseback. Neighbours went about their business and new settlers passed by once towards their chosen lots. On a rare occasion one might spot that pathetic soul from the fringes of civilization, the solitary pioneer trudging millward mile upon mile with a sack of grain slung across his shoulders, later to pass homeward with the grists therefrom. Perhaps a dozen times a day people would pass by—hardly a crowd, but the pedestrious pace allowed time to exchange greetings and news. Along with the contacts made through family outings, such meetings contributed to minimizing the loneliness and drudgery which was always so near at hand in a region newly settled.

Beyond the Neighbourhood

The commercial function of the pioneer farm must not be overlooked, although it accounted for only a tiny fraction of the off-farm trips made by any one household. A man who had four hundred bushels of wheat to send to market in one year was passing beyond the pioneer phase, but it would take no more than ten wagonloads to remove the whole lot. One or two hundred bushels were more characteristic.[16] Yet, because the export of grain was so intimately tied to the survival of the community, and because it involved long trips, sometimes several days in duration and concentrated into brief portions of the year, it has the illusion of vast importance. The grain trade gave a road definite reason to be the width of a wagon, and a wagon box, mounted either on wheels or sleigh runners, was probably as commonplace on farms as the horse to draw it. Speed really did have some importance in grain-export circles, as good sleighing conditions might not be counted on for more than scattered days over ten or twelve weeks.[17]

It was at the commercial level that the first signs of a hierarchy of routes was becoming evident. From every port along the Lake Ontario shore a road led inland, connecting with the imperfect grid of farm access roads. Along these feeders the farm wagons or sleighs made their way to the "spinal column", heading directly to the lakeshore. These so-called main roads were structurally indistinguishable from the others in almost all cases. In fact, they may actually have been worse than many after a day of supporting a steady stream of laden farm wagons from the back country. Any temptation to choose a parallel, alternate route was mitigated, however, by the presence along the main roads of one very important rural feature: the tavern.

Taverns and inns made the trip to "the front" bearable for team and teamster alike. Forty miles of freighting a day was possible only over snow and ice, and was exceptional.[18] Even at that pace, no farmer inland more than twenty miles could get out and home to sleep again without a night on the road. For many, putting up for more than one night was normal, and frequent refreshment stops *en route* were essential for all. One or more taverns every six or seven miles became characteristic in southern Ontario by the 1830s.[19] Earlier there may have been fewer establishments exclusively in the business of serving the travelling public, but their place was taken by farms along the way, where a family would gladly sell a drink (doubtless home-prepared) and water the team.

The lakefront town was the metropolis for the farmer-settler, and the nearest he probably ever got to the outside world. It may have seemed quite impressive if his destination was Toronto, *primus inter pares* of the Lake Ontario ports, but Cobourg, Darlington, Oakville, and dozens of others had very little to show for being commercial hubs. There was the lakeshore road and the inland road intersecting at a junction presided over by a blacksmith shop, a dry-goods store, the post-office, possibly a newspaper office, and two or three inns where the men off the wagons rubbed elbows with those in from the boats. Board siding over a wooden frame was characteristic, with perhaps an older log building covered to match.[20]

There was Port Street, or Navy Street—names given to the stub running down to the wharf itself—flanked with warehouses, a chandlery perhaps, a woodyard, and the customs house. On the other side, these places faced an embayment of the lake or the estuary of the stream which commonly formed a part of such ports. A platform-like ferry stood by to take lakeshore road traffic across the river-mouth in the open season; the ice served as a bridge in winter, and during freeze and thaw, shoreline communications were suspended. The mill was a few hundred yards inland where the estuary ended and waterpower was available. Schooners or barges could sail up for direct loading. Perhaps a schooner stood at the wharf or, if the visitor came on the proper day, he might see one of the two or three steamboats which plied the British side of Lake Ontario in the 1820s. Around, in seemingly haphazard alignment, stood an assortment of houses ranging from a pretentious frame or stone mansion of the entrepreneur who made the town, to the modest storey-and-a-half of a shipmaster, to the cabin of the barman, stable-hand, or farmer on the edge of the built-up area.

That was it: perhaps two hundred people in some of the larger places and all tied into the export trade in one way or another. The flour mill or warehouse was the end of the known world so far as the farmer was concerned, but it made good sense for him to venture forth this far. Bringing his own few wagon-loads of grain to the lakefront gave the farmer perhaps ten percent more remuneration for his grain than at the barn door and, at the same time a chance to buy imported goods off the boat before the mark-up levied at his neighbourhood general store further inland. There was also the chance of receiving cash, even if to a lesser face value than credit at the mill for remuneration in goods at the miller's store.[21]

After transacting his affairs, the farmer began his retreat by way of the tavern, into the hinterland. Behind, out across Lake Ontario, lay the strange and impersonal world of merchants and middlemen, business newsletters, customs officers, locks and canals, the open sea. Ahead was one's own bailiwick—a dozen square miles in which faces and vistas were known personally even if witnessed only infrequently. After the last winter load it could be months before a man came to the front again to catch another glimpse of the edge of the outside world. So too in every port hinterland up and down Lake Ontario, and thus the little isolated units would remain for the duration that an export-based economy predominated.

Transportation was an essential, yet unobtrusive, part of the landscape of early Upper Canada. It was very much a matter of personal concern, exemplified most clearly by the farmer driving his own grain, in his own wagon or sleigh, drawn by his own team, to the outside market. The settler cleared trees off the road allowance in front of his land not because some ineffectual law said that he must, but because he needed to get somewhere. The same self-serving purpose prodded him into clearing in front of wood lots along the route to market. Sometimes a farmer would need to borrow oxen or a sleigh, but usually the work with them would be carried out by himself. Only when it took several men working together to accomplish a particular task did larger groups get together, and then only for the benefit of the one landholder.

By the 1840s more and more attention was being given by township and county authorities to local communications. Their interest in roads and bridges beneficial to areas larger than any one man's immediate neighbourhood was assisted by an increasing number of cash payments by farmers who were wealthy enough to pay off their road duties, rather than work them off [22] Rights-of-way were ditched and trees removed well back from the driving surface, so that a visible swath ran through a forest. Cuttings, embankments, and bridges all were evidence of efforts far beyond the parochial interests of one man. It was a short but logical step to corporate involvement in transportation, first in the form of plank road companies and then railroads. These developments produced the specialist who served the transporting needs of the agricultural community on a full-time basis: the hotelier, the toll-keeper, the freight agent, the train crews, and so forth. Carters appeared at the barn door to transport the grain of the farmer now engaged in a crop and livestock economy which took all his time. Any trips he made to town were with the family, in the carriage, for shopping or social reasons.

In the early days, many of the assets of transportation were inconspicuous because they served other functions as well. This was particularly true in the clearings, and was one of the reasons that one can talk about the pioneer woodsman's life and never mention transport at all. Oxen disappeared into the woods or pastured with the other cattle when their work was done; farmers and families turned into porters and teamsters as occasion demanded. The duties became more distinctive with generations after the first. As oxen became redundant, their places were taken by both light horses of no special breed, for carriages and riding, and by heavier teams to do the plowing or freight carting.

Earliest Ontario was not a land of the wheel. Stone boats looked like casually-placed wooden boxes which gave no clue as to their basic function except when actually in use. Dragging operations called for no vehicles at all, and only the ox-yoke and chain hanging in the barn hinted at how transporting had taken place. Only later on in the farm-making era did a fleet of rolling stock take its place in the barn and transform that building into a running shed. Shelters for carriages behind country churches date back no further than the end of the pioneering phase and, at that, families invariably found the roads far below their growing expectations of comfort. [23]

Early Upper Canada had among its distinctive characteristics a particular set of transportation facilities. Later generations would work out their relations with transportation and be similarly well-served, but never with the degree of subtlety presented to the observer of the Ontario landscape as first settled.

Notes

[1] For examples of approaching transportation change by modes, see George R. Taylor, *The Transportation Revolution* (New York, 1952), chapters 1-7, and George P. de T. Glazebrook, *A History of Transportation in Canada*, rev. ed. (Toronto, 1964), chapters 3-5. For a discussion of the relations between settlement and provision of access, see Albert Fishlow, *American Railroads and the Transformation of the Ante-Bellum Economy* (Cambridge, Mass., 1965), especially chapter 4.

[2] See Richard L. Morrill, *The Spatial Organization of Society*, 2nd ed. (Belmont, California, 1974), pp. 170-80, for a brief discussion and bibliography on the subject.

[3] Of 100,000 occupiers of land in 1851, 87,000 were in agriculture. Approximately 150,000 of the 950,000 people reported in Upper Canada in 1851 were in urban places of 1,000 or larger. *Census of Canada, 1851-52*, 2 vols. (Quebec, 1853, 1855), vol. 1.

[4] For details regarding the constantly-changing land disposal system in Upper Canada, and its effect upon the distribution of settlers, see Lillian F. Gates, *Land Policies of Upper Canada* (Toronto, 1968), especially the summary, pp. 303-07.

[5] John Howison, *Sketches of Upper Canada* (London, 1821), p. 248.

[6] Censuses between 1826 and 1841 had categories for oxen, cows, and "other cattle", in 1842 and 1848 for neat cattle only, and in 1851 and 1861 for oxen, cows, and calves. The actual numbers tabulated show oxen and horses in equal proportions and rising numbers until the late 1830s, but by 1861 oxen were outnumbered by horses four to one. Prior to the 1840s they made up one-quarter to one-third of all cattle, but were down to less than ten percent in 1861. Canada, *Census for 1871*, Vol. 4 (Ottawa, 1876), *passim*.

[7] Howison, *Sketches, op. cit.*, p. 253.

[8] Anna Jameson, *Winter Studies and Summer Rambles in Canada*, Vol. 3 (London, 1838), p. 227.

[9] In 1834, only one million acres were "under culture" of five million "occupied," for example. Considering the large quantity of crown land ungranted, the cultivated acreages ranged from less than five percent to rarely more than twenty in any one township. *Census for*

1871, p. 114. In 1851, 3.7 million of 9.8 million acres occupied were under culture. *Census for 1871,* p. 194.

[10]Glazebrook, *History of Transportation, op. cit.,* pp. 110-11.

[11]On any topographic map of southern Ontario at a scale of 1:50,000 appear road deviations which date from the time of original settlement. Many were confirmed and others eliminated in cases placed before the District Courts of Quarter Session, particularly during the 1830s.

[12]Original in the Canadiana Gallery, Royal Ontario Museum, Toronto.

[13]W. H. Smith, *Smith's Canadian Gazetteer . . .* (Toronto, 1846), p. 81.

[14]Archibald Lampman, "Heat", lines 6-12, in A.J.M. Smith (ed.), *The Book of Canadian Poetry* (Toronto: Gage, 1943), p. 176.

[15]Assessment ledger books through the nineteenth century had a column for entering the tax against carriages and carriage horses.

[16]Four hundred bushels of wheat was the production of some 16 to 20 acres which, in a rotation of wheat alternate years or less frequently, suggests more than 40 acres in farm, or the work of ten to fifteen years to clear. The best source on the details of rotations, rates of farm-making, and so on, is Clarence H. Danhof, *Change in Agriculture: The Northern United States, 1820-1870* (Cambridge, Massachusetts, 1969), *passim.* For an example of the juggling of figures necessary to make estimates of the correct order of magnitude, see Thomas F. McIlwraith, "The Logistical Geography of the Great Lakes Grain Trade, 1820-1850", unpublished Ph.D. dissertation, University of Wisconsin, Madison, 1973, pp. 92-114.

[17]A discussion of the circumstances leading to heavy hauls in winter and early autumn appears in Thomas F. McIlwraith, "The Adequacy of Rural Roads in the Era before Railways: an Illustration from Upper Canada," *The Canadian Geographer,* Vol 14 (1970), pp. 356-57.

[18]Samuel Strickland, *Twenty-seven Years in Canada West,* Vol. 2 (London, 1853), p. 194.

[19]Edwin C. Guillet, *The Pioneer Settler and Backwoodsman* (Toronto, 1963), p.120, citing unidentified sources.

[20]Descriptions and paintings of towns abound. Some general remarks appear in Jacob Spelt, *Urban Development in South-central Ontario,* rev. ed., Carleton Library Series (Toronto, 1972), pp. 52-53, and fuller descriptions of major cities in Frederick H. Armstrong and Neil C. Hultin, "The Anglo-American Magazine Looks at Urban Canada on the Eve of the Railway Era", Ontario Historical Society, *Profiles of a Province* (Toronto, 1967), pp. 43-58. Watercolours by James P. Cockburn, P. J. Bainbrigge, H. F. Ainslie and William H. Bartlett depict many of the smaller lakeshore towns; see examples in Michael Bell, *Painters in a New Land* (Toronto, 1973), pp. 12, 106,

108, 127, 130, 146. Bartlett's sketches have been reproduced as
engravings in Nathaniel P. Willis, *Canadian Scenery* (London, *ca*.
1840).

[21]A recently-completed study which says a good deal about merchant activity is T. W. Acheson, ''The Nature and Structure of York
Commerce in the 1820s'', *Canadian Historical Review*, 50 (1969), pp.
406-28.

[22]Evidence of this transition may be found in such a source as the
Home District bylaws for the years 1845-49.

[23]McIlwraith, ''Adequacy of Roads,'' *op. cit.,* pp. 357-58.

5. THE IMPACT OF NINETEENTH CENTURY AGRICULTURAL SETTLEMENT ON THE LAND

Kenneth Kelly

This paper presents an overview of the impact of nineteenth century agricultural settlement on the land of Ontario. It must of necessity be brief and sketchy, for the investigation in this province of the changing evaluation of resources, the effect of settlement on soils, vegetation, hydrology and climate near the ground, and of the evolution of various cultural landscapes is just beginning. The first part of the paper deals with man-environment relationships and the second with the succession of agricultural landscapes.

The following scheme, developed by this writer, outlines the general sequence of man-land stances in nineteenth century Ontario.[1]

1) An initial settler evaluation of land.

2) The initial planned modification of the sites judged acceptable for settlement.

3) The recognition of a range of adverse effects of these modifications. Together with changed socio-economic goals and broadened market demand, this gave rise to

4) The conceptualization of new, ideal or efficient agricultural landscapes, and

5) The planned remedial modification of the land resource base, and the adoption of new agricultural practices, to implement these ideals.

The initial settlers' evaluation of land, until about 1850, was in terms of its capability for wheat production and the costs of development. The judgment of both soil and site was based on the character of the tree cover. Settlers believed that the very worst soils for wheat were those under pure stands of pine. Where oak and chestnut, beech alone, or beech and maple dominated a site, they found that the soil was light and gave only small yields. A mixture of hardwoods and pines indicated at best a fair or fair-to-poor soil for wheat. Many of the settlers' guides asserted that the lands under softwoods other than pine were rich and would produce good wheat harvests, but this evaluation was the subject of controversy. In contrast, there was general agreement that a mixed hardwood cover indicated a prime soil for wheat. In judging land, settlers also considered the amount of time and money required to bring the site into cultivation and the amount of immediately cultivable space per acre this investment would produce. Assessed in these terms, the land under oak-chestnut and beech-maple were deemed good for the initial settlement of poorer immigrants. Although the wheat yield was low, its quality was high, Furthermore, these sites were easy to clear, for there were very few trees to the acre, and there were no wet patches on this well-drained land. However, after a few years, yields dropped to an unacceptable level as the thin layer of forest mould was dissipated; then, commonly, settlers abandoned their farms and moved on to other sites. The mixed hardwood lands were reputed to produce high wheat yields over the long-term. They were harder to clear because of their denser tree cover. More stumps remained after clearing and the fields often had seasonally wet patches on them, reducing the amount of immediately cultivable land. Nevertheless, the task of developing these lands was not beyond the means of average settlers, and sustained high yields made them the choice sites for most would-be farmers. The wet, heavy lands dominated by cedar, tamarack, and hemlock, although often judged as having the richest soils, were avoided by most settlers. To develop their high potential productivity their occupants not only had to clear, but also to stump, level, drain, and even deep plough these sites.[2] In some areas settlers selected their land by a different system. They simply located themselves close to a highway which led to a market centre. This gave rise to a "ribbon" pattern of initial settlement. Such a pattern appears to have developed along Yonge Street in York County and, later, along the colonization roads of the Muskoka District. In Simcoe County, which lies between these two areas and which was settled after the one and before the other, the distribution of early farms coincides with that of mixed hardwood and beech-maple lands.

When a settler had selected a site for his farm,[3] his first planned modification of it was to clear away the trees. This was designed to remove the competition to his crops for light and nutrients. It was several years after clearing that the settler turned his attention to the removal of stumps, tree roots, and stones from his fields. The stumps and roots of most hardwoods rotted out after five to seven years, after which the farmer could plough out the roots and take away the stumps with little effort. At the same time he usually removed the surface stones from his fields. Pine stumps took many more years to rot. Before the opening of railroads, which facilitated the spread of stumping machines, the settler had to chop and burn out the pine stumps.[4]

The artificial drainage of the small wet patches which occurred on land formerly under mixed hardwoods could begin after stumping and rough levelling. Its purpose was to carry off the water which otherwise would lie on the land for much of spring until evaporated by the sun's heat. There are some indications that the old English clay land draining technique of building ridges and furrows with the plough was used on some of Ontario's heavy lands. But the wet patches on the loams and clay loams were drained by the cheaper of the then new British methods. Farmers dug trenches and partly filled them with brushwood, stones, or planks before replacing the earth. Tiles were just coming into use by 1850, but still were relatively uncommon in 1880. Underdraining not only increased crop yields on these lands but also, in effect, lengthened the spring sowing and cultivating season. The pace of small scale artificial drainage increased after mid century. Railroad construction widened the availability of labour saving machinery. Many farmers had cleared much of their land and thus could apply more effort to drainage work. Above all, a strong demand had developed for spring sown crops. Farmers found it to their advantage to take steps to facilitate spring sowing; the under-draining of wet patches was one such step.

Farmers could undertake small scale, piecemeal draining unaided, although they commonly failed to secure and develop a proper outfall. The inception of large integrated projects, however, required financial and legislative aid from the provincial government. Effective legislation finally materialized between 1869 and 1873, based on British experience. Large scale drainage can be interpreted as a remedial modification of the land and will be discussed later in that context.

Almost immediately after clearing some of their land for crops, settlers discovered that they had created niches for weeds. Formerly minor constituents of the forest flora—wild lettuce, choke cherry, raspberry, sumach, and aspen poplar —invaded the fields, choking out the crops and dominating abandoned land. Thus, native weeds became an important component of the early agricultural landscapes of the province. They became less of a problem with the expansion of clearings and after several decades of biennial naked fallowing.[5] But as they receded they were reinforced by exotic, Old World weeds introduced by settlers in improperly cleaned consignments of crop seeds. These probably included various thistles, wild mustard, and couch grass. They spread through the cultivated lands and, with some of the native weeds, found permanent places in the landscape, on cut-over land, on poorly managed grassland, and among the fences and stone piles which marked field boundaries.

It took farmers longer to discover other unlooked-for effects of deforestation. However, by the 1880s many were aware of a change in the run-off: percolation ratio. Clearing caused dissipation of the forest soil's organic layer, allowing more rainwater to run off immediately and less to percolate into the soil. Many springs and creeks dried up entirely during the summer, while rivers carried less water at this season than formerly. The increased surface run-off of both rain and melting snow also caused flooding to previously unheard of levels. Moreover, soil erosion, by 1880, had become serious along the lake fronts and noticeable on the steeper of the more recently cleared lands. Farmers became aware of increased summer drought. Some, at first, incorrectly attributed this to a supposed reduction in total rainfall or change in its distribution following deforestation. But most ascribed it to the lack of shelter, which allowed the parching winds a broader sweep over the land. Farmers also recognized that the lack of shelter in winter caused serious damage to fall-sown wheat, grass, and orchard crops. Furthermore, the protecting snow which now was blown from the fields tended to be dumped in drifts across the highways, making winter travel and freighting difficult. Finally, farmers complained of increased winter cold as winds howled around their barns and houses, raising the cost of both living and livestock production. The darker, obverse side of small scale, piecemeal drainage also became apparent during the last quarter of the century. It increased and accelerated surface run-off, commonly resulted in the flooding or waterlogging of adjacent lower lying land, and occasionally caused the deposition of debris on neighbouring fields.

The agricultural literature had warned settlers that they would exhaust the land rapidly unless they practised improved farming. Many of the fragile soils originally under beech-maple and oak-chestnut did decline rapidly in productivity. However, the question of whether, during the era of wheat farming, any significant area of the richer loams or clay loams was exhausted to the point of making wheat farming unprofitable is underinvestigated and very much open to debate. There are assertions in the travellers' literature and some of the settlers' guides that this, in fact, did occur. At the same time there are isolated records of farmers taking a wheat crop from a given field each year or every second year, without any use of manure, for several decades and still getting satisfactory yields. Such allegations and reports add a dimension to the question, but do not provide any conclusive answers. Annual estimates of wheat yield by township are available for some parts of Ontario from the early 1850s to 1880. Some of these records show only irregular fluctuations in fall wheat yields between 20 and 30 bushels per acre. They reveal no decisive downward trend culminating in unremunerative levels. In other areas, fall wheat yield did fall fairly steadily over a period of 20 to 25 years, down from about 30 to below 10 bushels per acre. However, in most cases this decline was followed by a quite sharp rise. Fluctuating yields resulted largely from weather conditions, but serious declines over many years were accompanied by complaints that the available wheat varieties were degenerate and infested by diseases and insects. A sustained rising trend in wheat yields seems to have followed the introduction and acceptance of a new, vigorous variety and the termination of a cycle of insects or disease. This does not, of course, prove that richer lands were not significantly depleted, merely that wheat yields were affected by several variables. After mid-century profitable markets opened for many farm products. As a result many farmers diversified their operations and thus were able to follow a "scientific" rotation involving more manure. While pursuing short-term profit, they incidentally took some steps to maintain soil fertility. Other farmers—perhaps those on the poorer or longer settled lands—shifted in large numbers to dairying, feed farming, or stock raising. This withdrawal of less productive lands from wheat cultivation and the reduction of the frequency of wheat cropping on the good land inevitably increased the average yield for the township as a whole. Agricultural change, then, may have concealed some of the effects of actual soil depletion. Soil exhaustion dropped out of the literature as a key issue after the early 1870s. In part this may have been because the problem was receding, but in part it was because summer drought and winter kill now seemed more obvious and immediate threats to wheat production

The conceptualization of efficient, new agricultural landscapes developed out of these perceived threats to continued prosperity as well as in response to the demand for a wider range of farm products and changed socio-economic goals.[6] Agricultural settlement had produced an overcleared landscape which was judged unsatisfactory on economic, ecological, and perhaps also on aesthetic, grounds. The efficient general agricultural landscape visualised by the 1880s was to have a substantial woodland component. Furthermore, it was to show no trace of the grain monocultivation of earlier days, for only mixed—or at least a highly diversified—agriculture was regarded as progressive. "Modern" agriculture raised livestock and livestock products (sometimes alone and sometimes in combination with cash grains) and it produced and used substantial quantities of manure. Finally, the new landscape was to provide land and work for some of those who, at the moment were leaving their farms and moving into the towns or out of the province. The abandoned light, fragile lands were judged irredeemable for agriculture and the sandy outwash plains useless (tobacco was not yet an important crop) and in fact these soils were earmarked for reforestation. Those parts of the Canadian Shield which had been colonized by farmers were being re-assessed in the 1880s as fit only for sustained yield forestry. However, it was generally felt that swamp and marsh lands could be developed at low cost as the last "internal frontiers" of the province, halting or reducing rural depopulation and stabilizing the rural tax base.

The remedial modification of the land took three basic forms: the diversification and "improvement" of agriculture; reforestation; and the drainage of swamps and marshes. Discussion of agricultural change will be deferred until later in the paper. With regard to reforestation, the development of woodlots and shelter plantings around the house and barn resulted from the unaided efforts of individual farmers. In contrast, farm boundary and highway plantings were subsidized by township and provincial governments. Although many farmers were unwilling to make investments in reforestation from which they themselves would get no return, these components of the new general landscape did appear in some areas during the late nineteenth century. However, the large forest preserves on the sandy outwash plains which figured so prominently in the new landscapes envisioned by government agencies did not materialize until well into the twentieth century. The draining of marshes and swamps proceeded rapidly during the 1870s and 1880s. The greatest progress was made in the southwest, but smaller areas were reclaimed throughout southern Ontario. This was made possible because an appropriate legal and technical framework had been developed in Britain and transferred to Ontario and because, again following the British example, the provincial government aided in the financing of these large scale drainage projects. Thus new agricultural landscapes were created—flat, productive farmlands with open main drains and straightened, "managed" stream courses, often ringed with dykes and pumping stations. However, the enthusiasm for this large scale reclamation disappeared with the onset of agricultural depression in the late 1880s and early 1890s. Thereafter, for the most part, swamps and marshes remained as permanent gaps in the agricultural settlement pattern.

Farmscapes and Agricultural Landscapes

The impact of agricultural settlement was, of course, wider than that outlined above. It gave rise to a series of evolutionary sequences of cultural landscapes. It is not the intention here to discuss the evolution of townscapes or of the components of the general landscape associated with transportation although they developed partly in response to the needs of farmers. The final part of the paper will concern itself only with farmscapes and agricultural landscapes. Farmscape connotes the visual appearance of an individual farm. It is defined in terms of crops on the land, the amount of forest cover, fences, gardens, buildings and yards, stumps and stones remaining on the fields, and the like. As a settler developed a given type of agricultural enterprise from a forested site, he created a series of farmscapes which moved progressively from the pioneer farm to the fully established enterprise. Moreover, in response to market changes, the farmer often progressed from one type of enterprise to another. During the first half of the nineteenth century there were at least three agricultural traditions in southern Ontario: wheat farming, feed farming and improved farming. Each of these was developed through a distinctive series of stages, and each stage presented a different farmscape. After mid-century, as a wider range of farm products came into demand, agriculture in general was diversified and became more mixed. A farmer could diversify to a degree while remaining within his original agricultural tradition, but at some point he left it and embarked on farmscape building within the new mixed farming tradition.

The term farmscape has been employed thus far because, from the evidence of a detailed study of the agricultural evolution of Simcoe County,[7] it appears that individuals engaged in, say, wheat farming did not all progress at the same rate; nor were all parts of even a small area settled simultaneously. Thus, in detail, a single township often exhibited a complex mosaic of farmscapes. Indeed, for at least the three decades after mid-century, agricultural landscapes—regions comprising a sizeable block of farmscapes which were reasonably uniform in appearance—existed only in a very loose sense. Thus, in Simcoe County from the early 1850s well into the 1870s, there were two general agricultural landscapes: a grass dominated feed farming one in the northeast; and a wheat dominated one in the south and northwest. In both, however, the actual farmscapes could span the gamut from pioneer to mixed farming.

An outline of the visual appearance of the land at the various stages of development within the wheat farming tradition can be constructed on the basis of the Simcoe County evidence.

1)   The early settler, or pioneer, farmscape.

The cleared area was small, most of the lot remained under forest. The one or two small fields were stumpy, untidy, and unlevelled. They were under a wide range of crops, reflecting a diversified subsistence economy, which were choked and overtopped by recolonizing forest plants. The only fences were trees felled in line along the edge of the cleared land and roughly trimmed. Because harvests were small there were no real barns. Livestock were raised, but no accommodations were provided for them. For most of the year they foraged in the forest, and during winter they picked around the land being cleared. Most houses were simply rough shanties. In districts settled before 1830 a pioneer agricultural landscape developed, and persisted for many years, as it did also whenever settlers penetrated remote areas and consequently found themselves isolated from markets. In most areas, however, the pace of agricultural development was so rapid that pioneer farmscapes lasted only a few years.

2)   The early commercial wheat farmscape.

This developed directly out of the pioneer farmscape and, as a result, initially shared some of its features. Lines of felled trees commonly marked the boundary of the clearing; but rail fences (usually in the snake form, for this required no wire or nails) separated one field from another. For many years the fields continued to harbour stumps and stones, and the old, original shanty remained—although now it was used for storage or to house poultry. Weeds of recolonization remained a severe threat to the crops. For this reason only about half of the cleared land (excluding the small subsistence plot) was under wheat; the rest was in biennial naked summer fallow. The fields were somewhat irregular in shape and varied considerably in size. Because of enlarged grain production, barns had made an appearance, and with increased prosperity more substantial frame or log houses had become the norm. The problem of recolonizing by forest plants persisted for many years, and for virtually two decades the only significant commercial demand was for wheat. Consequently, an early commercial wheat landscape developed in many of the older settled parts of southcentral Ontario in the years just before mid century. There were, of course, variations from one farm to another in, for example, the amount of land cleared, the degree to which the fields were free from weeds of recolonization and from stumps, and whether or not the artificial drainage of wet patches of land had begun.

3)   The post-railroad commercial wheat farmscapes.

During the 1850s local marketing agencies developed to express the broadened external demand for farm products, and railroads reduced the costs of bulk transportation. Those early commercial wheat farmers who had progressed furthest in the improvement of their land could take immediate partial advantage of the new opportunities. Farmers with capital, or access to credit, could take even greater advantage. They began the underdraining of seasonally wet land in earnest; they stumped, removed the stones from, and rough levelled their fields to permit the use of labour saving machinery; and they re-organized their field boundaries better to follow the four- to six-course rotations of diversified agriculture (often at the same time replacing the snake with the more efficient straight rail fence). Insufficient work has been done to permit a precise description of the various post-railroad commercial wheat farmscapes, but the following will serve as an illustration.

Initially some farmers who had beaten back the weeds of recolonization dispensed with the naked summer fallow but continued to employ two-course systems. They alternated wheat with either peas or clover and timothy. Many farmers by-passed this "stage", and others moved rapidly beyond it to four- or six-course systems in which grain crops were alternated with peas, clover and timothy, and sometimes roots.[8] Thus the occurrence of monocultivation was diminished as was that of naked fallowing for cleaning the land. This visual change was accentuated as farmers substituted oats or barley for one of their wheat crops. In another style of development, a few farmers turned to continuous grain cultivation after the need for biennial fallowing was past; but, for a variety of reasons, this agriculture did not survive long in any area. The earliest diversified agriculture in Simcoe County was cash crop oriented. However, with the opening of marketing agencies for cattle and sheep (which came relatively late in this county) many farmers began to turn, in a small way, to livestock production and fattening. Oats now were consumed on the farm, roots were grown in larger quantities, and grass occupied each field for two consecutive years (as meadow during the first year and as pasture during the second). Storage facilities for feed became more conspicuous, and yards and buildings for the winter accommodation of livestock made an appearance. All farmers intensified and diversified their agriculture. How far they went was a function of the interplay of many factors including the capital or credit and the size of the labour force at their disposal, and their ability to use labour-saving machinery. Thus, a mosaic of post-railroad commercial wheat farmscapes developed; and scattered through it were the farms of men who, in the pursuit of maximum short-term profit, had progressed to mixed farming.

Feed farming had a different origin and developed through different stages. In the northeast of Simcoe County the basic initial demand expressed was for hay to supply the lumber camps, not for wheat for the external market. Moreover, agricultural settlers could find part-time work in these same lumber camps. They took one wheat or potato crop from newly cleared land and then sowed it down with clover and timothy. This grass cover protected the cleared land quite effectively from recolonization by forest plants, and with a much smaller labour investment than that required by biennial naked fallowing. In addition, farmers obtained a crop from each field every year. Thus the initial farmscape was heavily dominated by grass. After it had occupied a field for several years, the meadow was very much reduced in value because of infestation by couch grass. However, lands formerly under hardwoods could be ploughed, thoroughly cleaned, and re-seeded when, after five to seven years, the stumps and roots had rotted. Many farmers in fact did re-seed. But as settlement, and the cleared area, increased others turned to the cultivation of peas and especially oats as well as hay. This raised their income per cleared acre, although at the cost of a greater labour investment in agriculture. This was a reasonable course of action because, with an increased population, every farmer could not also work in the lumber camps. As the effects of railroad construction and new, intermediary marketing agencies were felt in the northeast, many farmers found it advantageous to diversify their operations still further by producing also for external markets. Some grew a little wheat or began the raising and fattening of livestock, others did both. Gradually, a number diversified their operations to the point that they left feed farming and began the pursuit of mixed agriculture.

Although the third quarter of the nineteenth century was characterized by mosaics of farmscapes rather than agricultural landscapes, the foundations of new agricultural regions (and, therefore, of landscapes) were being laid. The later stages of development within the wheat, feed, and improved farming[9] traditions often produced similar farmscapes; and the three streams of agricultural development ultimately coalesced in mixed farming. It seems very likely that, during the last quarter of the century, agricultural landscapes re-emerged. Very little work has been done on this topic, and nominal censuses (the bases for the identification of farmscapes and for the denial of the existence of agricultural landscapes between 1850 and the mid 1870s) are not available after 1871. Nevertheless, it is not hard to imagine the development of a broad pattern of agricultural landscapes, perhaps resembling the distribution of farming regions established from 1880 township statistics by Reeds.[10] Fragments of evidence suggest that agricultural landscapes of this kind were forming in Simcoe County during the late 1870s. By 1880 farms were well established over much of southern Ontario, and farmers were becoming aware of the need to take steps to maintain the productivity of their lands. The era of high input farming—using pesticides, herbicides, and large quantities of artificial fertilizers—had not yet begun. Thus, the way to maintain productivity lay in the so-called scientific rotations and the production and use of manure. Mixed agriculture, which raised several products and which integrated livestock raising with cultivation, became the rule. There were, however, many improved or scientific rotations and several types of mixed farming. The pattern of agricultural landscapes which emerged reflected most clearly the distribution of land types and also the distance from major market centres.

Notes

[1] This scheme, or conceptual framework, was one of the results of an examination of marginal lands in nineteenth century Ontario supported by grants from the Ontario Department of University Affairs.

[2] Kenneth Kelly, ''The Evaluation of Land for Wheat Cultivation in Early Nineteenth Century Ontario'', *Ontario History*, LXII (1970), pp. 57-64.

[3] Although most early settlers seem to have been reasonably careful in selecting farm sites, a number bought land unseen and found themselves in very unsatisfactory locations.

[4] Most stump fences away from the immediate fronts of Lakes Erie and Ontario date from the post-railroad period.

[5] For a detailed description and explanation of biennial naked summer fallowing see Kenneth Kelly, ''Wheat Farming in Simcoe County in the Mid-nineteenth Century'', *The Canadian Geographer*, Vol. XV (1971), pp. 95-112.

[6] Examples of changing socio-economic goals can be seen in the promotion of import substitution agriculture and of new staples during the 1850s and 1860s, as well as in the drive to provide recreational facilities and havens for wild life, and the concern about the declining level of living of agricultural settlers ''stranded'' in worked-out lumbering areas, which formed some of the bases for the reforestation movement of the 1880s and 1890s.

[7] Kenneth Kelly, ''The Agricultural Development of Simcoe County, Ontario, 1850-1880'', unpublished PhD thesis, Geography, University of Toronto, 1968, and subsequent, as yet unpublished, research.

[8] Some farmers who still had a large weed problem could control it economically after mid-century without biennial fallowing if they were able to use labour-saving machinery both to hoe roots and peas as they grew and to bastard fallow after their grass crop. However, many lagged a little behind their more fortunate neighbours in intensification and diversification because they were compelled to employ a naked summer fallow once in the course of each rotation.

[9] The evolution of improved farming after 1850 has not been investi-

gated. For a discussion of improved farming during the early nineteenth century see Kenneth Kelly, ''Notes on a Type of Mixed Farming Practised in Ontario During the Early Nineteenth Century'', *The Canadian Geographer*, XVII No. 3 (1973), pp 205-219.

[10]Lloyd G. Reeds, ''Agriculture Regions of Southern Ontario 1880 and 1951'', *Economic Geography*, Vol. 35 (1959), pp 219-227.

6. AN INTRODUCTION TO FOREST EXPLOITATION IN NINETEENTH CENTURY ONTARIO

C. Grant Head

Harold Innis, Arthur R. M. Lower and other workers in economic history have emphasized the important role that export products have played in the Canadian economy.[1] During the third quarter of the nineteenth century, our main period of interest in this paper, products of field agriculture and of the forest comprised some three quarters of the total exports of Upper and Lower Canada[2] and, as we will point out below, these products were highly specialized.

Although the quantity, quality and spatial organization of agricultural production—particularly in Upper Canada—have received considerable attention from historical geographers, these aspects of forest exploitation have not.[3] Yet the value of forest products exported compared very favourably with that of agricultural products. In the years between 1849 and 1866, for example, while field agriculture contributed just less than $190 million to the export coffers of the Canadas, forest exploitation supplied just less than $180 million. From when reliable statistics begin in 1849 until 1860, there were only two years when field agriculture out-produced forestry.[4] Indeed, in earlier years, wood exports overshadowed all others; in some years in the mid-1830s, they made up three-quarters of Canada's total exports.[5]

The two endeavours were highly specialized: agriculture and forestry relied heavily on one plant species each. In 1860, a representative year, more than $9 million of the something more than $14 million earned by export field agriculture was from wheat and flour, while $8 million of the $11 million earned by forest exports was from squared pine timber, planks, boards, and deals, these latter mainly pine, almost certainly (Figure 6.1 shows the dominance of pine in 1871, when statistics are more easily available).[6]

Essentially, then, we can characterize the export trade of the Canadas of the third quarter of the nineteenth century as one relying upon wheat and pine. A comparison of Figures 6.2 and 6.3 emphasizes that these exploitations were spatially complementary. Each, furthermore, had different implications for the developing landscape.

Two major and distinct types of operation can be recognized in Canadian forest exploitation in the nineteenth century: the use of trees for "squared timber" and the use of trees for "saw logs" and thus planks and boards. These two processes were contemporary, but as the century progressed the former production became overshadowed by the latter, and early in the twentieth century squared timber faded completely from the scene.

Squared Timber

With difficulties of supply to Britain from the Baltic during the Napoleonic wars, tariff preferences for timber were given to British North America, and major supply houses quickly established here. Although first attentions were to the Nova Scotia and New Brunswick areas, entrepreneurs had begun to harvest the Ottawa River district before the end of the first decade of the nineteenth century, and within another decade attention had extended as far as the areas along the St. Lawrence and about the eastern end of Lake Ontario. This meant large gangs of men in the woods each winter to cut and square the trees, teaming of the huge sticks to the major rivers, assembly into rafts where rivers widened or met lakes, and final marshalling and loading on specially-constructed timber vessels at Québec City (Figures 6.4 to 6.6).[7]

In the areas with direct access to the Ottawa and Upper St. Lawrence Rivers, this attention was big business—indeed, *the* big business. Something like ninety-eight percent of all squared timber produced in the Canadas came from Upper, rather than Lower Canada, and it was the Ottawa River country that was the dominant area.[8] In 1845, for example (and in this, typical of the 1840s at least), somewhere around eighty percent of all squared

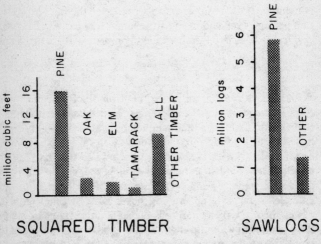

6.1　Species utilization in Ontario's forest industry in 1871. *Canada Census 1871.*

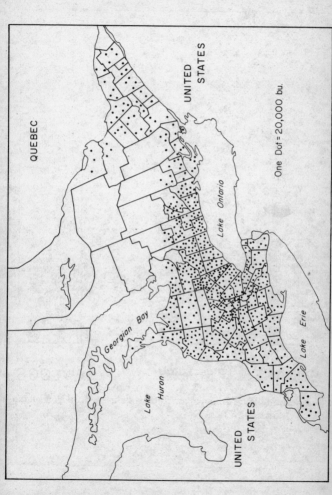

6.2   Wheat production in Ontario, 1871. One dot represents 20,000 bushels harvested. *Canada Census 1871.*

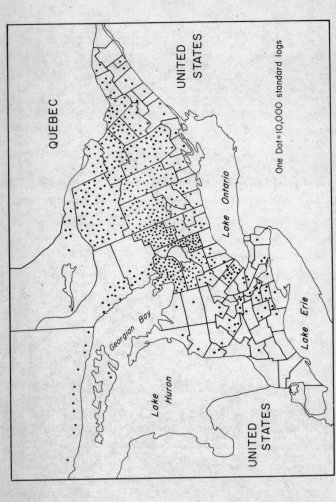

6.3 Pine sawlogs harvested in Ontario, 1871. One dot represents 10,000 standard logs. *Canada Census 1871*.

6.4　Squaring pine at the fell site with broad axe. Courtesy Ontario Ministry of Natural Resources, Historical #166.

6.5　Shooting St. Lawrence rapids with a portion of a squared pine raft. Photo from Calvin Co. records, courtesy Queen's University Archives.

6.6   Timber core at Quebec City. Courtesy Public Archives of
      Canada, C4776-A.

timber produced in the Canadas came from this watershed and
its tributaries (Figure 6.7).[9]

Other districts did produce squared timber, but it was a small
amount when compared to the hundred thousand and more
sticks coming from the Ottawa Valley each year. By 1871,
squared pine exploitation was still very much concentrated in
the Upper Ottawa district (although with an outlier of activity in
northern Simcoe County on Georgian Bay—Figure 6.8), and it
is likely that the Ottawa district remained, until the end, the
heart of the squared timber harvest in Upper Canada, or Ontario.
Production in Southern Ontario along Lakes Erie and Ontario
was smaller, and encumbered with extra charges for towing or
schooner transport along lake waters—operations unnecessary
in the rapidly moving rivers of the Ottawa district.[10]

Sawn Lumber

While the demand for squared timber did not slacken even after
the removal of British tariff preferences before mid-century,
there was very little trend to an *increase* in demand. Instead, the

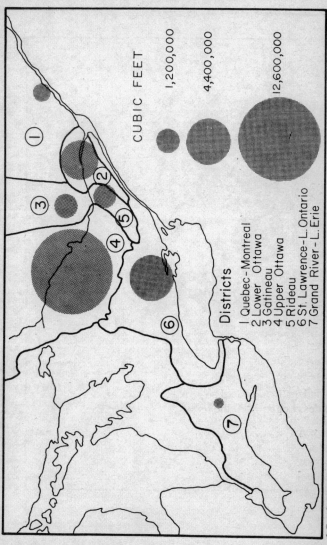

CUBIC FEET

1,200,000

4,400,000

12,600,000

Districts
1 Quebec–Montreal
2 Lower Ottawa
3 Gatineau
4 Upper Ottawa
5 Rideau
6 St. Lawrence–L. Ontario
7 Grand River–L. Erie

6.7 Squared timber harvested, by district, 1845. From Canada, *Journals of Legislative Assembly, 1846.*

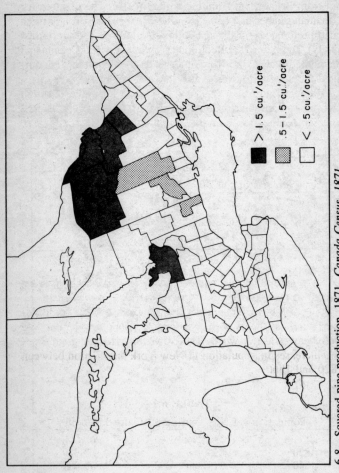

> 1.5 cu.'/acre

.5 – 1.5 cu.'/acre

< .5 cu.'/acre

6.8 Squared pine production, 1871. *Canada Census, 1871*.

growing demand was for sawn lumber, and this demand came
not from Britain, but from the United States. The clamour for
Canadian lumber had come even before the removal of British
tariff preferences for the squared product (1842-1851, progressively), and before the Reciprocity Treaty between Canada and
the United States (1854), two pieces of legislation that encouraged the new trade even if they did not begin it.

Example figures for the flow of Canadian lumber through
Oswego (a particularly significant import point for the United
States) that illustrate the rapid growth of this trade are given in
Table 6.1, below.

TABLE 6.1

Imports of Canadian Lumber at Oswego[11]

1840	2,000,000 feet
1846	6,000,000 feet
1849	44,000,000 feet
1850	60,000,000 feet

Three main reasons underlie this increase in trade in sawn
lumber to the south.[12]

1. A rapidly growing demand in the United States for building materials. Cities were growing at phenomenal rates and
were heavy users of wood. Table 6.2 illustrates the great absolute increases in population in New York and Boston between
1820 and 1860.

TABLE 6.2

Populations of New York and Boston, 1820-60[13]

	New York	Boston
1820	124,000	43,000
1840	313,000	93,000
1860	814,000	137,000

2. Accessible stands of pine, the preferred building wood,
were exhausted. In the United States, only Maine and Georgia
really offered significant stands and these were facing rising

logging costs. (In the mid-west, Chicago and other cities were preying on Wisconsin forests.)

3. A developing inland water transportation system was directing Canadian lumber to the eastern United States markets. The Rideau Canal allowed Ottawa Valley material to come to the Lake Ontario port of Kingston. Small canalization schemes, slides and other works fed logs and lumber from the country immediately north of Lake Ontario to that lake's northern ports, and the Welland Canal connected Lake Erie ports to Lake Ontario. In all of this, Oswego was the important pivot that fed Canadian lumber down to the Erie canal system and to the major wholesaling focus at Albany, New York.

The pattern of activity, therefore, that had for the squared timber operations been so strongly focused on the Ottawa, now emphasized more the ports on the north shores of Lakes Ontario and Erie, particularly the former. The quantities of planks and boards exported at each Ontario port for 1851 and 1867 are shown in Figures 6.9 and 6.10.[14] A comparison of the two maps suggests the areal effect of increased demand. Many ports contributed a significant proportion to the export in 1851, but by 1867 a concentration of exports in the ports from Brockville to Toronto is notable as is a dropping-off of volume from Lake Erie ports. Particularly significant is the growth of exports at Port Hope and Toronto, at each of which the expansion from 1851 to 1867 was about three times that of the general provincial expansion in plank and board export.

Although the focus of export activity was the north shore of Lake Ontario in the third quarter of the nineteenth century, the actual places of both forest harvest and of sawing became increasingly far from these ports. Census data on the number of hands employed in saw mills tell us something of the nature and distribution of this activity in 1851 and 1871 (Figures 6.11 and 6.12).[15] The 1851 pattern is one of small saw mills (2.3 hands/mill) located in the counties strung along the shores of Lakes Erie and Ontario. We lack data, but we suggest that these were mills utilizing a relatively local resource, one intermixed with the agricultural activity. We suggest that logs were not brought long distances to the mills and it is evident that sawn lumber did not have far to go to point of export. The pattern in 1871 was essentially similar to one established by 1861 and

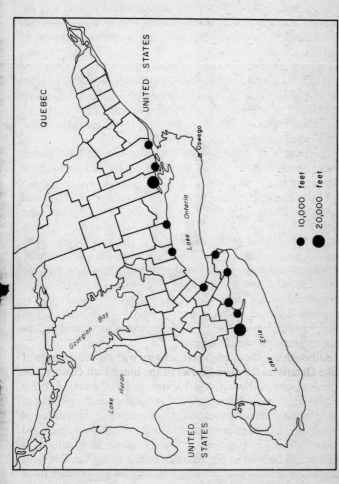

6.9 Export locations of planks and boards, 1851. Canada, *Journals of Legislative Assembly*, 1853.

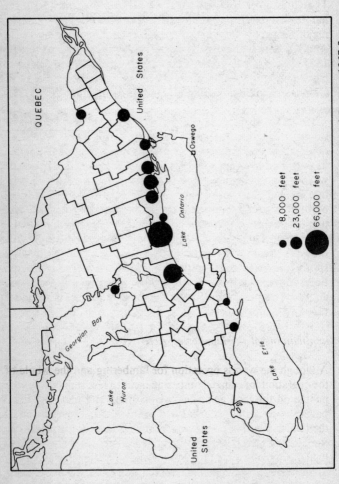

QUEBEC

United States

Oswego

Lake Ontario

8,000 feet

23,000 feet

66,000 feet

Georgian Bay

Lake Huron

Lake Erie

United States

.10 Export locations of planks and boards. 1867 Canada *Sessional Papers*, 1867-8.

significantly different to that of 1851. The average mill by 1861 and 1871 employed nearly three times as many men as in 1851. The Ottawa (or Bytown) area, which employed insignificant numbers of men in sawmilling in the 1851 census, had become a major centre by 1861 and was even more important by 1871. And whereas the lakeshore counties dominated the picture in 1851 it was those areas some distance back from the lake, particularly in a broad arc from Ottawa through the Bay of Quinte area to Simcoe County, that were important by the later years.

By 1871 we have statistics on location of harvest of pine sawlogs (Figure 6.3).[16] With the exception of a few interesting outliers, the concentration of harvest appears as a rough ellipse, its ends tied to Ottawa on the east, and Simcoe County on the west. A most instructive comparison is between this map of harvest and the map of sawn lumber export in 1867 (Figure 6.10).[17] A strong transportation link between raw material and point of export is obvious and a factor of great importance in the geography of lumbering. For the supply of logs to the mills, this link was usually provided by streams utilized during the short spring freshet. From the mills to the port of export, however, the finished product demanded navigable waterways or railways, and improvement of the former and the appearance of the latter was an ongoing process.

Implications of the Lumbering Activity

Although the woods operation for lumbering and the whole of the operation for squared timbering meant a less stable pattern of people on the land and a less geometrical and less long-lived pattern of communications than did agriculture, other aspects of the total lumbering operation did have significant implications for lasting geographical imprints. The railway lines employed to haul the manufactured products to the distributing and exporting towns were one example. As competition rationalized the transport routes, of course, some of these were abandoned, but some also have survived to the present. Investments in steamboat and lockage systems on the waterways were oriented to forest exploitation, and these items and their effects were also long-lived. Whereas the manufacturing process associated with

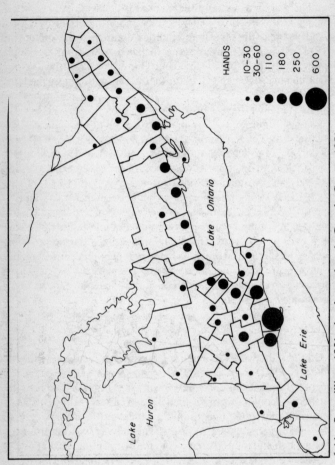

HANDS

10–30
30–60
110
180
250
600

6.11 Sawmilling, 1851—hands employed. *Canada Census 1851.*

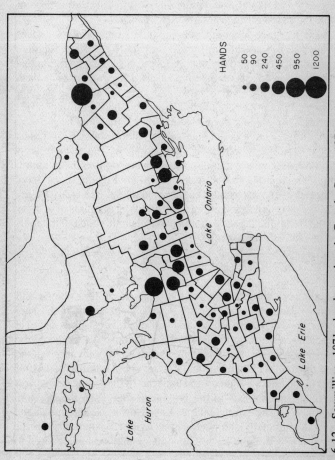

HANDS

50
90
240
450
950
1200

Lake Ontario

Lake Erie

Lake Huron

6.12 Sawmilling, 1871—hands employed. *Canada Census 1871.*

squared timber was largely in the United Kingdom and very little in Canada, that for sawn lumber was located here and often gathered a settlement around it. And the settlement, by generating within itself additional functions, was to be more permanent than the saw mill that initially spawned it.

Finally, since squared timbering utilized relatively few trees in a stand, but logging for lumber took much of what it found in a mixed age or relatively mature forest, the latter operation had considerable effects on the forest itself. Large amounts of slash left added to the fire hazard, and large areas were heavily burned. In many areas where sawlogging had been important, the forests were just as much cleared as if they had been put to agricultural use. The clearing for agriculture was recognized as a step to neatness, efficiency, and progress, and such agricultural clearing would in most cases be so recognized even today. But the clearing that resulted from sawlogging must have shocked even nineteenth-century minds, and can today be described only as a desecration. The following accounts of activity in the Belleville Agency should make clear this and other details of the forest exploitation.

THE "ONTARIO" OR "BELLEVILLE" AGENCY

There were three administrative regions of the Woods and Forests Branch of the Crown Lands Department in Canada West, or Ontario, in the second half of the nineteenth century: the Ottawa Agency, the Belleville or Ontario Agency, and the Western Agency. Activity in the Belleville Agency through the last third of the century usually ran at about a third to a half of that in the Ottawa Agency and until the 1870s these two districts were the major ones in the province; after 1886 the Western Agency (southwestern Ontario, Lake Huron, Georgian Bay and west) completely overshadowed activity anywhere else in the province.[18] It is the Belleville Agency that we have chosen to examine in this pilot study.

Trends in Squared Timber and Sawlog Harvests

From the statistics we are able to use, it is evident that the Belleville Agency fitted well into the general provincial trend to sawlogs and sawn lumber production. Figure 6.13 compares the Agency's estimated outputs of both sawn lumber and squared timber, and illustrates how, particularly after the first few years of the 1860s, the former production increased markedly.[19] The figures we have for one major operator, Mossom Boyd of Bobcaygeon, confirm and strengthen this suggestion: while the order of Boyd's squared timber production did not change from the early 1860s to the early 1870s, his sawlog production increased approximately ten-fold.[20]

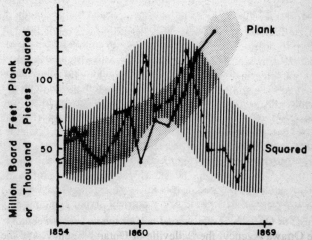

6.13   Outputs of squared timber and sawn lumber in Belleville Agency, 1854-69. For sources see footnote 19, Chapter 6.

Patterns of Licensing and Harvest

The pattern of forest exploitation within the Belleville Agency is shown only in part by the general map, Figure 6.3, for operations within the agencies themselves reveal a tendency towards major local concentrations of forest operations.

Licensing.   Early in the 1850s in the Belleville Agency (and in the Ottawa, slightly previously) a relatively comprehensive licensing system was introduced for cutting on public lands. Before winter operations began, operators applied to the Crown Lands Department for exclusive permission to cut upon certain desired areas, usually defined by township, lot and concession. For this right, the operator paid a fee—after 1851, 2s. 6d. per square mile, after 1866, 50 cents per square mile plus an initial fee of $4 per square mile. Upon each licensed area (no single license covered more than fifty square miles in unsurveyed townships and twenty-five square miles in surveyed townships) a specified minimum cut was required each year or the license fee—the ''ground rent''—for that operator and that area would double for the next season, until it reached the amount that would be paid on that area as production duties had it been exploited to a specified minimum level. This cumulative doubling of ground rents was intended to reduce speculation in licensed areas. All operators were entitled to renewal of licenses provided they complied with regulations, but competition for new or vacant berths was solved at different times either on a ''first-come, first-serve'' basis or by issuing to the operator paying the highest ''bonus'' at auction.[21]

The pattern of licensing in the Belleville Agency, shown in Fig. 6.14, then, represents the pattern of *interest* by operators in the area's forest resource.[22] It is far more extensive and inclusive in coverage than would be a pattern of actual exploitation. But even so, it indicates in much greater detail the patterns of attention than do general Ontario statistics, and begins to point up the local concentrations of activity and their changes over time. Most notable is the band-like form, that coincides in very general terms with the southern edge of the Canadian Shield. Through the nearly twenty years represented here, however, while the eastern end of the band remained firmly fixed on the Rideau Lakes area north of Kingston, the western end swept rapidly northwards. By 1871, the licensing had reached as far north as it possibly could in the Belleville Agency, for it had reached the limit of the Lake Ontario watershed, and beyond was the licensing of the Ottawa Agency (not shown here) which had advanced from the northeast. The pattern and its movement through time resembles a wave of interest moving inland from

Lake Ontario, refracted by early contact with the watershed boundary in the east, and rushing northwards in compensation in the west. As the wave advances, however, it does leave certain concentrations of activity well established: the adjacent townships of Kaladar and Kennebec in the east (about thirty miles north of Napanee) are a continuous focus of interest, as are those north and east of Bobcaygeon in the western section.

Harvest.   The mapping of actual production by townships (Figure 6.15) reveals the local concentrations of activity even more clearly.[23] The pattern of pine sawlogs for 1854 shows the emphasis on this production in the eastern portion of the district, north of Napanee and Kingston. The squared timber, however, was coming from the districts not yet heavily exploited for sawlogs—in the west, the townships focussing on the Kawartha Lakes, and in the east the most northerly townships of the watershed. Squared timbering usually preceded sawlogging in an area.

The lower set of maps in Figure 6.15 shows a pattern of exploitation in a period of general economic depression, 1855. A lighter harvest is evident, and the places of harvest are more scattered. Some squared pine appears to be coming from essentially agricultural lands on the lakefront where perhaps costs are lower. Figure 6.16, the pattern of pine sawlog harvest in 1871/72, reveals an even greater concentration of exploitation.[24] Evidently, by this date, although the pattern of *licensing* was one that was widely spread over the district (Figure 6.14:1871), nearly half of the *harvest* came from only four adjacent townships. This may have been due to accessibility, resource, or other factors; we do not yet know.

Patterns of Individual Operators

Mapping of the aggregate woods activity of all operators in the agency, by townships, has exposed a tendency to concentrate upon certain blocks of townships. One might logically extend this tendency to suggest that individual operators would also confine their activites to one area, and keep their operations compact even within that area. The great expense involved in transporting supplies to woods sites and in preparing streams

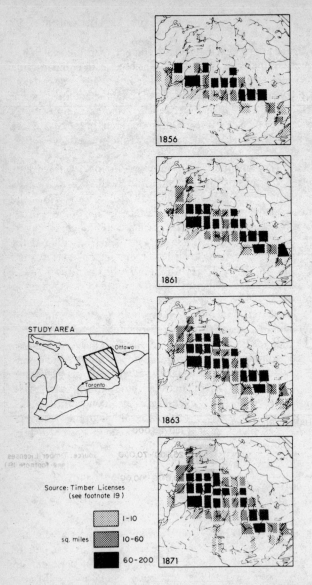

6.14 Licensing of timber cutting, Belleville Agency, 1856, 1861, 1863, 1871. From computer map print-outs. Sources: footnote 19.

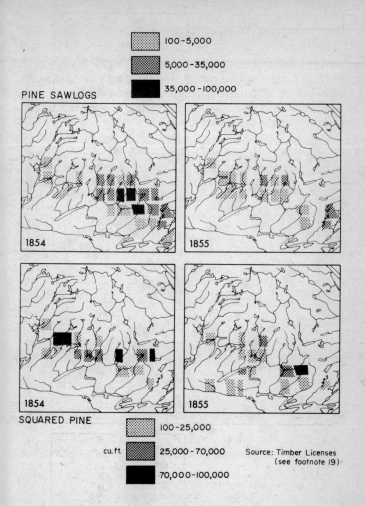

PINE SAWLOGS

100-5,000

5,000-35,000

35,000-100,000

1854

1855

1854

1855

SQUARED PINE

100-25,000

cu. ft.   25,000-70,000

70,000-100,000

Source: Timber Licenses
(see footnote 19)

6.15   Production of pine sawlogs and squared pine Belleville Agency,
        1854, 1855. From computer map print-outs. Sources:
        footnote 19.

for a log drive would suggest this approach (see Figures 6.17 and 6.18). The expected pattern, however, is not found to be the case. Indeed, the tendency of the larger individual operators was to disperse their operations over several townships and to several sites within these townships.[25]

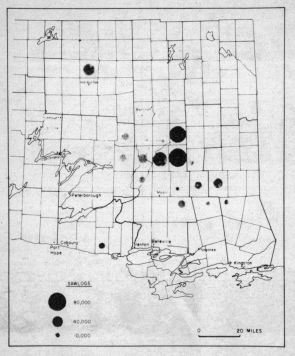

6.16   Pine sawlog harvest, Belleville Agency, 1871-2. Courtesy
        Ontario Archives, Woods and Forest, F-II-5, Vol. 3.

Figure 6.19 illustrates the cutting pattern, by township, of the Mossom Boyd Company during the winter of 1872/73.[26] Operations were dispersed amongst five townships. The significant point to note is that each operation fed into a separate stream branch. Even within heavily-used townships, individual operators spaced their operations widely. Figure 6.20 shows the operations of the Rathbun Company in Lake Township in

6.17   One method of getting logs past swamps or rapids was the use of slides. Courtesy Public Archives of Canada, C27212.

6.18   An alternative to the slide was the flooding of obstacles through the use of dams; a slide would be necessary in addition below the dam. Courtesy Public Archives Canada, C21203.

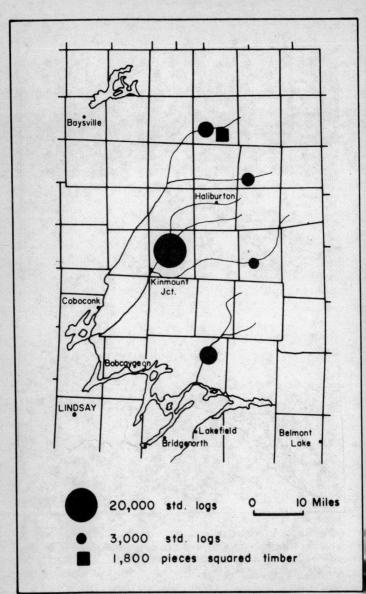

Baysville

Haliburton

Kinmount
Jct.

Coboconk

Bobcaygeon

LINDSAY

Lakefield

Belmont
Lake

Bridgenorth

20,000 std. logs   0   10 Miles

3,000   std. logs

1,800 pieces squared timber

6.19   Mossom Boyd: production, 1872-73. Courtesy Public Archives
Canada, 'Boyd Collection', Vol. 383.

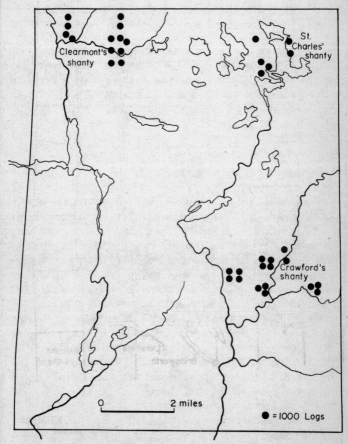

6.20 Rathbun: production in Lake Township, 1873-74. Courtesy Ontario Archives, Woods and Forests, E-5, Vol. 4.

1873/74, and shows its three shanty locations.[27] As in the previous map, one can note that each shanty feeds into different streams.

One answer to this dispersion of shanties by operators is found in a reading of the company documents. The spring log drive was uncertain. Sometimes particular streams, especially the smaller ones, failed to flush out as expected, and much of a season's cut for that shanty was therefore kept back. No operator could afford to risk his year's supply of raw material by relying upon one stream alone. Uncertainty of supply in the headwater streams encouraged a dispersion of risks.

DISCUSSION

It has been demonstrated that the exploitation of the forest was a major industry in nineteenth century Ontario. Its effects, however, were felt even in places removed from the bush camps and the saw mills. The harvest of the pine required a considerable labour supply, and this was drawn from the agricultural communities to the south of the Shield, and in some part from Canada East, or Québec. The historical literature suggests that the Shield-edge farmer engaged frequently in logging to supplement the agricultural earnings from his land.[28] In the Ottawa Valley, the French-Canadian woodsman has become a legend, but even in the Belleville Agency the seasonal import of this additonal labour is indicated. About a third of Mossom Boyd's men were of French-Canadian origin, and we know of some examples of his specific recruitment from those parts. The hotels and boarding houses that handled this seasonal ebb and flow of men were prominent features of the Shield-edge settlements such as Bobcaygeon, Buckhorn, Fenelon Falls, and Lakefield (Figure 6.21).

The men and their work animals, furthermore, required significant quantities of food. Each local woods operation—the "shanty"—that employed some thirty or so men for about five months each year, required the following major supplies:[29]

Pork — 36 Bbls.	Hay — 20 Tons
Beef — 10 Bbls.	Oats — 400 Bags
Flour — 34 Bbls.	Chop — 400 Bags
Potatoes — 76 Bu.	

6.21   The ebb and flow of lumbermen at Shield-edge hotels: Forest
       House, Bobcaygeon. Courtesy Public Archives Canada,
       C27220.

In the Belleville Agency in the early 1870s, there were
probably approximately eighty shanties in operation for the
sawlog harvest alone.[30] To supply these shanties, then, in
addition to minor needs, some 32,000 bags of oats, like amounts
of chop, nearly 3,000 barrels of pork, like amounts of flour,
more than 6,000 bushels of potatoes and 1,600 tons of hay
moved annually over long rough-chopped trails to the site of
operations deep in the woods. Some of these supplies were
obtained locally; probably all of the hay was grown within
twenty or so miles of the logging operation, and probably much
of the chop and oats came from somewhere within the local orbit
of the forest-oriented towns. How much this demand helped
support a local Shield-edge farming until the collapse of the
forest exploitation in the area is a question yet to be investigated
in depth. We know, however, that Boyd's pork, at least, came
from as far away as Chicago.
    We have alluded above to the effects that saw logging had

6.22   The landscape after lumbering: near Kinmount, late nineteenth
century. Courtesy Public Archives Canada, C21238.

upon the exploited forest. Even in the upper areas of watersheds
touched most lightly, logging took most of the commercial
timber, and the slash so generated and left on the forest floor
contributed to massive uncontrolled burnings. In the areas
closer to mills, the little resource left after the major commercial
exploitation of the 1850s and 1860s was picked over again and
again, for pieces that would earlier have been called short or
defective, for fence posts, and for species ignored in the rush for
pine. These areas burned too. In the Trent River watershed north
of the Kawartha Lakes in 1912, less than one acre in ten was not
severely cut over, recently burned, or slowly recovering from
the effect of burn. Only about one percent of the total area
contained immediately-exploitable softwood.[31] Figure 6.22
shows an area near Kinmount, about twenty miles north of
Bobcaygeon, towards the end of the nineteenth century.

Finally, the exploitation of the forest in the Belleville Agency
laid down a pattern of investments in transportation and settlement that outlasted its original function (Figure 6.23). Mossom
Boyd, for example, was the driving force behind the settlement
at Bobcaygeon, was the president of the Trent Valley Naviga-

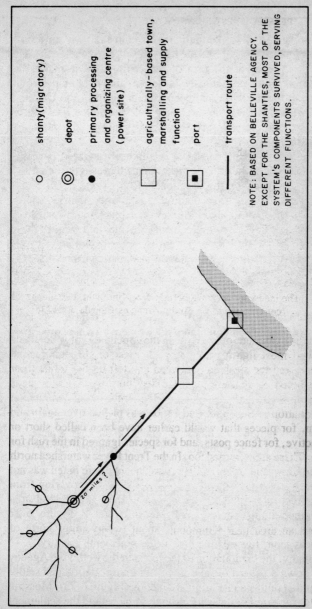

○   shanty(migratory)

◎   depot

●   primary processing
     and organizing centre
     (power site)

☐   agriculturally-based town,
     marshalling and supply
     function

■   port

——   transport route

20 miles ?

6.23   The general pattern of forest exploitation, as suggested by the Belleville Agency.

tion Company, and was similarly involved in a railway towards the Lake Ontario ports.[32] As the forest resource dwindled in the Belleville Agency at the turn of the century, these material investments were consciously turned to the exploitation of tourists. A few of these had been coming in from the United State for sport fishing, and as this publicity filtered back, the lumbering entrepreneurs and others supported it with printed advertising.[33]

The railway lines that had taken out lumber brought in tourists to Lakefield and Lindsay, the steam-boats that had pushed out barges of lumber took the vacationers to the same hotels and boarding houses that had accommodated the woodsmen at Fenelon Falls, Buckhorn, Mount Julian, and other places on the Kawartha Lakes. Except for the woods shanties and some of the depots, then, the settlement pattern of forest exploitation was largely preserved in the exploitation of American tourists.

CONCLUSION

The exploitation of the forests of Southern Ontario was an activity of major economic importance to the province, producing export earnings similar to those of field agriculture through many decades of the nineteenth century. The productions of squared timber and sawn lumber were both significant in different times and places, but it was the latter activity that had the greatest impact upon the landscape.

The impact of cutting, sawing and exporting the forest trees was both upon the visual landscape and upon the spatial pattern of settlements and transportation routes. Logging left the forest heavily culled, and uncontrolled fires fed easily and widely upon the waste. The exploitation left perhaps the majority of the source area barren, at least temporarily. And southerly, along the most efficient routes for shipping and processing logs and sawn lumber, this enterprise established mill-oriented settlements and investments in railways and river improvements.

The effects of this forest exploitation of the nineteenth century, however, are little recognized today. Most of the areas culled and burned have revegetated, and although the species are now different, the impression is again one of boundless forest. The spatial patterns are seldom recognized as ones belonging to forest exploitation, since some components have disappeared completely and those remaining now serve another function, mainly that of tourism and recreation. Largely, the landscape of nineteenth century forest exploitation in southern Ontario is a lost one.

Acknowledgement

The financial assistance of the National Advisory Committee on Geographical Research of the Government of Canada is gratefully acknowledged.

Notes

[1]See, for example, A. R. M. Lower, *The North American Assault on the Canadian Forest* (Toronto, 1938); *idem.*, *Great Britain's Woodyard* (Montreal, 1973); H. A. Innis, *The Cod Fisheries* (Toronto, 1940), and *The Fur Trade in Canada* (Toronto, 1930); Lower and Innis, *Settlement and the Forest and Mining Frontiers* (Toronto, 1936).

[2]Canada, *Sessional Papers,* Session 1861, Appendix 2, Table 13.

[3]Some of the most relevant work on forestry is unpublished, and this paper owes much to the labours of these other people: Robie Bell, "Timbering [and Lumbering] in the Trent Watershed, 1850-1910", (seminar paper, Department of Geography, McMaster University); H. Pammett, "A Survey of Kawartha Lumbering (1815-1965)"; Graeme Wynn, "Settlement and Forest Exploitation in the Shield: The Ottawa Valley . . . ."; Mary Philpot, "Lumbering and Farming in the Bonnechere Valley 1830-1870: Complementary Ventures", B.A. thesis, Department of Geography, University of Toronto, 1973; and Michael Cross, "Dark Druidical Groves", Ph.D. thesis, University of Toronto.

[4]See Canada, *Appendices, Journals of the Legislative Assembly* and *Sessional Papers*.

[5]Lower, *Great Britain's Woodyard, op. cit.,* pp. 71, 261.

[6]The 1860 statistics are from same as in footnote 2; 1871 data from *Canada Census,* 1871, Vol. 3, pp. 224-231. The 1871 local anomalies from these attempts to generalize are perhaps even more interesting than the broad picture. Squared timber exploitations in woods other than pine were sharply concentrated in Essex, Kent and Bothwell (oak); Wellington North, Elgin, Glengarry, Prescott and Russell (tamarack); and Middlesex North, Oxford North and Huron North

(elm). Harvesting for sawlogs in woods other than pine was very much concentrated in Kent, Huron North, Essex, Elgin and Bothwell.

[7]See, for example, Lower, *Great Britain's Woodyard*, Part II, "The Anatomy of the Trade"; D. D. Calvin, *A Saga of the St. Lawrence, Timber and Shipping through Three Generations* (Toronto, 1945); and Philpot, ". . . the Bonnechere Valley. . . ."

[8]For example, Canada, *Journals of the Legislative Assembly*, Session 1846, Appendix T, Table G.

[9]*Loc. cit.*

[10]Calvin, *A Saga . . .*, makes this point, pp. 137-140, and also notes the risk of rafts breaking up in storms on the open lake. The costs show up in the "Boyd Collection", Public Archives of Canada (hereafter PAC), MG28, III, 1, Vol. 139, the journal of a trip with a raft in 1875.

[11]Cited in Lower, *North American Assault . . .*, *op. cit.*, pp. 101, 116 and rounded here.

[12]Most of this discussion on the reasons for the rise of the sawn lumber trade is from Lower, *North American Assault . . .*, *op.cit.*

[13]Cited in Lower, *North American Assault . . .*, *op. cit.*, p. 98, and rounded.

[14]From Canada, *Journal of the Legislative Assembly*, Session 1852-3, Appendix A., Table 22 and Canada, *Sessional Papers*, Session 1867-68, Appendix 1, Table 11. From 1865 onwards, these are specifically years ending on June 30; the bulk of the lumber was probably exported during the early part of this fiscal year, one calendar year previous. For simplicity, in this general discussion of trends I have applied the fiscal year dates as given in the offical tables without modification or qualification. Any more precise work must beware of the variations in fiscal and calendar years.

[15]*Canada Census, 1851-2*, Vol. 2; *1860-61*, Vol. 2, and *1871*, Vol. 3.

[16]*Canada Census, 1871*, Vol. 3.

[17]A neat presentation of the place of transportation and its changes requires data for 1851 and 1871 on places of harvest, of milling, and of export. We are forced to be less than direct in our arguments, because of missing data. Ticks in the cells below indicate data available.

	harvest	milling	export	
1851		√	√	
1871	√		√	(1867)

To fill both cells on milling, "hands in mills" can be used as a surrogate for the capacity of mills.

[18]Bell, "Timbering in the Trent Watershed . . .", *op. cit.*, Graph 7.

[19]Again, we are forced to make comparisons of general trends on graphs drawn from statistics gathered for differing purposes. We cannot use customs statistics to compare squared timber and sawn lumber exports for Belleville, since customs clearance for squared timber to a foreign market did not usually take place until the timber had reached Quebec City. Conversely, the Woods and Forests Branch did not tally sawn lumber being exported; this was done only by the customs authorities, at a number of points along the Lake Ontario shore, since most of it was going directly abroad (not via Quebec City) to U.S. markets. In short, statistics on squared pine export for the whole of the Belleville Agency are found in the "Clearance Registers" of Woods and Forests for Belleville, in Public Archives of Ontario (hereafter PAO), RG1, F-II-5, Vol. 2 (1854-1869), and the statistics for sawn lumber exports for the Belleville Agency are in the customs records for the ports that funnelled the Agency's production to the U.S.A.: Canada, *Appendices, Journals of the Legislative Assembly* and *Sessional Papers*, "Tables of Trade and Navigation", using the data for "planks and boards" exported from Belleville, Cobourg, Pt. Hope and Trenton.

A second problem is obtaining a rough comparability of the two graph lines of Figure 6.13. We can postulate that 1 cu. ft. timber = 12 bd. ft. less saw kerfs for cutting to planks, and therefore *1 cu. ft. timber equals about 10 bd. ft. planks*. (This does not agree with Lower's sliding scale—see Lower, "The Trade in Square Timber", *Contributions to Canadian Economics*; Vol. VI (Toronto, 1933), p. 60 or Lower, *Great Britain's Woodyard, op. cit.*, p. 258—which gives somewhat more board-footage to a cubic foot). But further problems are that the only consistently-used measure of squared timber cleared is "pieces", but a "piece" was not of standard size. Until someone comes up with a mean or mode cubic foot measure for a "piece", we will use a rough mean derived from Boyd Collection manuscript materials, *ca* 1870, of about *100 cu. ft. per piece*. For the purpose of balancing the two graph lines, therefore, we use:

1 piece timber = 1000 bd. ft. planks.

[20]The figures on which this statement is based are drawn from a wide range of booklets and papers in the boxes of the Boyd Collection. Within boxes the books and other papers are not separately catalogued or identified. It would be mere pedantry to account for each figure used in this general statement, but anyone who seriously needs the information may contact this author.

[21]This summary is meant to give an indication of what maps of timber licenses may mean, and glosses over the timing and details of changes in these regulations. For an introduction see R. S. Lambert and P. Pross, *Renewing Nature's Wealth*, Ontario Department of Lands and

Forests, Toronto, 1967, and especially their excellent bibliography. For details, one may consult Thos. Southworth and Aubrey White, "A History of Crown Timber Regulations from the date of the French Occupation to the year 1899", Clerk of Forestry, *Annual Report,* 1899 (Reprinted in *Annual Report of Lands, Forests and Mines,* 1907).

[22]Compiled from manuscript and printed licensing records. *1856*: P.A.O., RG1, F-II-4, Vol. 1 (Revenue Returns 1854-78) and Canada, *Journals of the Legislative Assembly,* Session 1857, Appendix 25. *1861 and 1863*: Canada, *Sessional Papers,* Session 1868-9, No. 6 (years 1861 to 1867). *1871*: Ontario, *Sessional Papers,* Session 1871-2, No. 41.

[23]P.A.O., RG1, F-II-4, Vol. 1.

[24]P.A.O., RG1, F-II-5, Vol. 3 ("Lumbering Operations"), 38-41; where the return has attributed a portion of an operator's cut to more than one township, and we have no other information, for the purposes of this map, I have simply assigned that portion of the cut to the first township named.

[25]These may be seen by plotting the licensing or cutting pattern for operators from the material cited in footnotes 16-18, above, for example.

[26]"Boyd Collection" (P.A.C., MG28, III, 1), Vol. 383.

[27]P.A.O. RG1, E-5, Vol. 4.

[28]A. R. M. Lower, *Settlement and the Forest Frontier*, pp. 44-47; Michael Cross, "The Lumber Community of Upper Canada, 1815-67", *Ontario History*, LII (1960), pp. 213-33; and Robert L. Jones, *History of Agriculture in Ontario, 1613-1880* (Toronto, 1946), pp. 109-121, 289-303. In Bonnechere, Philpot, *op. cit.*, felt that the farmers' major contributions to commercial forest exploitation were as labourers and haulers.

[29]Calculated mainly from "Boyd Collection", Vols. 103, 106, 107 and 383.

[30]Belleville Agency produced about 500,000 logs in 1871/72 (P.A.O., RG1, F-II-5, Vol. 3), and an average Boyd shanty produced about 6200 logs.

[31]Canada, Commission of Conservation, *Trent Watershed Survey* (Ottawa, 1913).

[32]See, for example, D. J. Wurtele, "Mossom Boyd: Lumber King of the Trent Valley", *Ontario History*, L (1958), pp. 177-189.

[33]See, for example, Grand Trunk Railway System, *Kawartha Lakes* (a booklet, timetable and accommodation guide, eleventh edition), Montreal, 1907.

Part II:
Some Special Contrasts
and Comparisons

. . . the industrious do very well but the 9/10ths that come out
are people who have not been industrious at home (to say the
best of them) and cannot well be expected to change morals
and manners and habits by a passage across the Atlantic.
(Lord Dalhousie, 1821, quoted by M. Cross, *Frontier Thesis*,
p. 68)

There was much greater variety in the people who moved into
Upper Canada than is intimated by Dalhousie's phlegmatic
opinion. The poor and not-so-poor of Europe, mingling with the
generally practical Americans, yielded a vigorous, many-
faceted, and probably unpredicted society by mid-century. It
was strongly marked by the comings and goings of population,
and gave the impression of being "exceedingly heterogeneous
and exotic . . . ; every body is a foreigner here; and 'home', in
their mouths, invariably means another country".[1] As a result,
there were at all times special contrasts and comparisons during
the period to which this book addresses itself; only a sample of
them appears in the following pages. Notable contrasts appeared between ethnic and religious groups, and many of these
have been particularly commemorated. Notable comparisons
began to appear between towns with a lake-port function (as
recorded, for example, in Smith's *Gazetteer*, 1846), while other
contrasts arose between such towns and inland nuclei based
instead on a road intersection and a growing agricultural hinterland. The contributions in Part II touch on these contrasts and
comparisons and on others inherent in Upper Canada.

Human settlement response to natural endowments has been a
perennial concern of Geography. In Upper Canada there were
many variations in the encouragement offered to settlers by the

environment, but there was no discouragement more dramatic than that of the Laurentian Shield. The edge of the Shield divides Peterborough County, and as one might expect, striking contrasts have been etched into the occupance of the county. The southern part of the county, with deep soils on the glacial drift materials, has become a successful farming area. The case of the Robinson immigration of poor southern Irish to this area is detailed by Brunger to show both some dynamics of migration and a story of agricultural success from rather unpromising beginnings. The northern part of the county lies on the Shield. Despite government assistance, such as in building "colonization" roads, this area has been engaged in a perennial struggle manifest in its steady loss of population, beginning by the fourth decade after settlement began. The few pockets of soil that existed on the Shield stood out because of their agricultural suitability, and gave particular emphasis to this rather basic man/environment relationship. The degree of restrictiveness by environment has a genuinely geographical expression: north of the Shield line only individual settlers were introduced, to scattered locations, whereas further south the Irish could and did settle as a sizable group.

After the settlement of Robinson's Irish, in 1825, and before the colonization roads of the 1850s and 1860s, reaching onto the Shield and toward the Bruce Peninsula, the western extremity of peninsular Ontario was opened to settlement. There an experiment was to be tried. It was to involve a land company, which was not new to British colonial settlement—there having been near-precedents along the Atlantic seaboard and elsewhere —but the company was to deal with the controversial chequerboard of remaining Crown Reserves and a block of new territory—The Huron Tract—which amounted to 1.1 million acres. The comprehensiveness of the company's operation, the acreage, and such a means of disposing of reserves, all were rather unusual items in the annals of Canadian land administration. The debate continues over whether or not the Canada Company was "a good thing" for the settlement of Upper Canada, but there is no doubt that via the Huron Road it spearheaded the advance to the Lake Huron shore. J.M. Cameron's paper considers the Canada Company specifically as a business operation engaged in resource development, and primarily in its relationship to its showpiece of Guelph and environs.

A settlement feature that only gradually began to make an imprint on Upper Canada was the growth of urban centres. This is not to deny that many of them began to grow spectacularly before mid-century, such as Toronto and Hamilton, and in fact began to draw numbers from the beginnings of the "rural-urban shift". But, during the era of Upper Canada, even the rapidly growing towns and villages primarily were in the service of the agricultural community. One nucleus that had an existence somewhat independant from agriculture was Kingston. Its roles as a military centre and then a transhipment point, camouflaged its growing dependance on an agricultural hinterland. As Osborne demonstrates, it was the truncation of its hinterland which led during the nineteenth century to the truncation of Kingston's influence.

There was a brash will to survive—indeed to prosper—in all sizes of urban centre in Upper Canada. The long-term prospects of villages apparently did have a great deal to do with the initiative and skill of individuals. Whether or not a desirable factory was enticed to put down roots, whether or not an attractive hotel was built, whether or not the railway established a station, all were linked to boosterism, and village vied with village to sell its potential for growth, often with little concern for either accuracy or cost. Ennals sets the rather representative competition between Cobourg and Port Hope in its ideological framework. A treaty with the Mississaugas in 1818 opened the land around and north of Rice Lake to settlement.[2] The battle for this hinterland, which stretched for about fifty miles beyond a corridor through the Oak Ridges moraine, raged for many years on the strength of a passionate and rather naive belief in the inevitability of Progress: change ultimately was always for the better, and cost, like terrain, was a difficulty to be surmounted. The towns in this case had both comparisons and contrasts. The most poignant comparison is that both towns, but especially Cobourg, carried the financial scars for decades after the substance of the competition had passed from popular memory.

Notes

[1]John Robert Godley, *Letters from America*, . . . 1844, quoted in G.M. Craig (ed.), *Early Travellers in the Canadas/1791-1867* (Toronto: Macmillan, 1955), p. 143.

[2]W.H. Smith, *Smith's Canadian Gazetteer* . . . (Toronto, 1846; Coles Canadiana Reprint, 1970), has a list of treaties, p. 243.

7. EARLY SETTLEMENT IN CONTRASTING AREAS OF PETERBOROUGH COUNTY, ONTARIO

Alan G. Brunger

This paper examines the settlement processes in two physiographically distinct areas of Peterborough County. Both areas were settled by Europeans during the nineteenth century although the more southerly area, characterized by thick glacial drift deposits, was occupied earlier than that to the north, located primarily upon the rocky Laurentian Shield. In describing the settlement, attempts will be made to generalize with regard to the locational decision-making involved and the factors affecting the settlers' assessments of place utility in the study area. The settlement of over two thousand Irish emigrants in the southern part of Peterborough County in 1825 was an event of great importance in the overall development of the region. The location of the Irish settlers is consequently examined in somewhat greater detail in the second half of the paper.

Migration, Settlement, and Place Utility

The process of settlement is the final stage of migration. Both result from individual decisions made by people who have decided to change their location of residence and livelihood. Such a change is often a major event in the life of those concerned and migration and settlement may be the result of considerable deliberation over a period of time. During this period the assessment of the place utility[1] by the potential migrant is a particularly important aspect of any subsequent decision to migrate. Place utility is assessed by each individual in regard to his present location and all known alternatives. It

117

forms part of the decision-making preparation prior to migration and involves the employment of all known information relating to the needs and satisfaction experienced by the person or persons concerned.

A drastic decline in place utility with regard to the occupied settlement site invariably leads to consideration of what Roseman has called "total displacement migration"[2] in which a relatively long move is made involving a disruption in the established pattern of life of those concerned. The direction of the move is usually to an area perceived at that time as having a higher place utility. The person may know the exact site of his destination although place utility is more likely to be assessed on a regional basis before the precise location is chosen. Selection of a site for settlement involves the selection of the most satisfactory location with the highest available place utility from the point of view of the individual settler. In total displacement migration categories of influences that may affect choice of both general area and site of settlement are, in order of declining importance, those of official control, livelihood, access and environment.[3]

Place utility may be assumed to have played a part in settlement decisions throughout human history. No basis exists for assuming that the factors that influence the assessment of place utility today were less important at earlier periods, although much less information may have been actually available previously on which to base a decision. The concept will consequently form the focus of description and interpretation of nineteenth century settlement in Peterborough County. In this way the several types of influence believed to affect place utility assessment will be identified and the local importance in aggregate settlement location estimated.

The primary question to be answered in the subsequent discussion is: what was the place utility of locations chosen for settlement? This may be re-phrased alternatively as: why did settlers select particular locations? At the present stage of knowledge if seems possible to answer this question in the general, if not in the individual, case.

The Peterborough County Environment

Peterborough County has a rectangular plan and is situated in east-central Southern Ontario (Figure 7.1). The physical geography of the county is easily divided into three regions: the interconnected Kawartha Lakes that are characteristic of the region, the rocklands north of these lakes, and the glacial drift area to the south. The Kawartha Lakes are glint lakes occupying for the large part a groove eroded along the junction of the Pre-Cambrian or Laurentian Shield rocks to the north and the gently dipping Palaeozoic strata overlying them and tilted southward. The junction neatly bisects the area of the county, extending from west-north-west to east-south-east as a serpentine line. The landscape either side of the junction owes much to the action of the Pleistocene glaciers which appear to have scraped off much of the material from the Shield and have virtually buried the Palaeozoic strata to the south beneath a mantle of drift, moulded in this area into hundreds of elongated hills called drumlins.

The area of Palaeozoic strata and parts of the Shield itself are covered by a varying thickness of glacial material which gives rise to a more complex subdivision of the physical geography.[4] Near the junction of the Shield and the younger strata, very little drift is found and limestone plains with quite shallow soils present a level and distinctive landscape. Locally, hills or outliers of younger strata form islands of level surfaced terrain in the sea of Pre-Cambrian rock. The latter is locally drift-mantled and thin soils have developed in such areas. The very resistant nature of the Pre-Cambrian rocks has hindered weathering and much of the landscape in northern Peterborough County is rugged rockland virtually free of soil.

The Kawartha Lakes form the major hydrological feature in the County although by no means constitute the only lakes there. On the southern margin is Rice Lake some twenty miles in length and on the Pre-Cambrian Shield are hundreds of smaller lakes. Many small streams traverse the northern area although it lacks major rivers to compare with those that flow over the Palaeozoic strata in the southern part of the County. Rivers such as the Indian and particularly the Otonabee form important

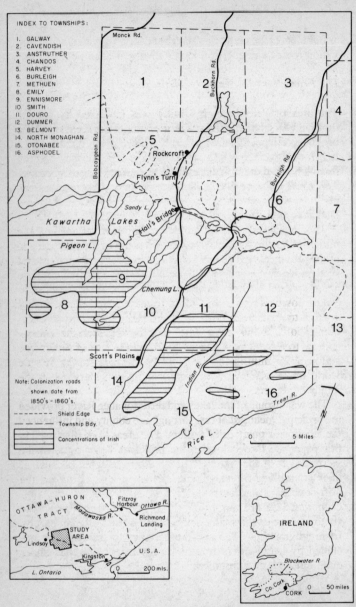

INDEX TO TOWNSHIPS:
1. GALWAY
2. CAVENDISH
3. ANSTRUTHER
4. CHANDOS
5. HARVEY
6. BURLEIGH
7. METHUEN
8. EMILY
9. ENNISMORE
10. SMITH
11. DOURO
12. DUMMER
13. BELMONT
14. NORTH MONAGHAN
15. OTONABEE
16. ASPHODEL

Note: Colonization roads
shown date from
1850's - 1860's.

- - - - Shield Edge
——— Township Bdy.
▤▤▤ Concentrations of Irish

0   5 Miles

Monck Rd.
Buckhorn Rd.
Bobcaygeon Rd.
Burleigh Rd.
Rockcroft
Flynn's Turn
Sandy L.
Hall's Bridge
Kawartha Lakes
Pigeon L.
Chemung L.
Scott's Plains
Indian R.
Trent R.
Rice L.
N

OTTAWA - HURON TRACT
Madawaska R.
Fitzroy Harbour
Ottawa R.
Richmond Landing
Lindsay
STUDY AREA
Kingston
U.S.A.
L. Ontario
0   200 mls.

IRELAND
Blackwater R.
Co. Cork
CORK
0   50 miles

7.1   Irish settlers, Peterborough County, 1825 (with later colonization roads) water links in the network of lakes and have provided communication routes and energy sources for the human population.

The Framework for European Occupance

The area of Peterborough County was inhabited by several thousand Mississauga Indians at the time of the creation of the province of Upper Canada in 1791. The land was obtained by a treaty of November 1818 and surveyors laid out the southern boundaries and the first township of the county in the same year. The county was subsequently divided into sixteen townships although the more northerly were laid out some twenty years later than those in the southern half (Figure 7.1).[5]

The inland situation of Peterborough County delayed the initial settlement by Europeans until the end of the third decade of the province's existence. In 1818 settlers appeared in several scattered locations in Smith Township and by 1820 in Otonabee and Asphodel.[6] Their locations were often riparian or as in Smith Township near an Indian portage route. Place utility appears to have been influenced primarily by access to communications at this early date. The isolation of the county appears to have been a serious brake on the rate of settlement and need for minimizing the problem of access to the outside world may well have been a paramount consideration in the minds of settlers.

The water route of the lakes and the Otonabee River provided the principal means of access through the county and influenced the location of many early settlers. The areas to be discussed in this paper are those close to the principal water route in the western half of the county. The areas are selected because of their contrasting physiographic character, one being on the drift-covered Palaeozoic rocks and the other on the Pre-Cambrian Shield, and for their distinct settlement history. The six townships of the southern area were those settled in part by Irish emigrants of 1825 and the northern townships were occupied by later settlers from a variety of backgrounds under quite different circumstances.

The Southern Settlement on Drift-covered Palaeozoic Strata

In the Otonabee River valley, the principal early route through the county, a few settlers had located on scattered sites during the period 1818 to 1825, in most cases close to the river. In 1820 Adam Scott built a modest saw and grist mill on the west bank of the Otonabee, where plains occurred, and utilized the power of a tributary stream for his mill.[7] Two retired British officers, R. Reid and T.A. Stewart, obtained land in Douro township on the east bank of the Otonabee in 1822 about two miles upstream from Scott. No other settlers occupied this particular township and for three years the Stewart and Reid families were the sole inhabitants. Their reasons for settlement in the region appear to have been partly the advice of officials who recommended they go to new townships where their relatively large grants could be obtained on contiguous lots. The lots actually selected were closest to the river in Douro township and proximity to this routeway appears to have been the reason for their selection.

In late 1825 the isolated and unpopulated nature of the Otonabee River valley and adjacent townships was abruptly ended by the settlement of approximately 2000 Irish emigrants. This group had been assembled and organized in Ireland by the Honourable Peter Robinson, a member of the Legislative Assembly of Upper Canada, who had been selected to superintend a scheme of assisted emigration of Irish paupers in 1825 in a role similar to that which he had carried out two years before. In 1823 he organized the passage of 571 emigrants who settled in four townships in Eastern Ontario about 150 miles east of Peterborough. In spite of considerable expense incurred in this initial scheme and subsequent debate over its relative success, parliamentary approval was given for a second emigration of Irish people under Robinson's supervision. The emigrants were to be selected from the same district in Ireland (Figure 7.1) as were those of the first migration and were to number 1500 in all. The task of selection was made difficult by the large number of applications and the political pressure from Irish land owners wishing to dispense with troublesome elements in their areas. When the emigrants finally embarked they totalled 2,024, in 306 families, ninety per cent of whom were from a relatively small area in the Blackwater River valley of County Cork.[8]

The emigration occurred throughout the late summer and fall of 1825 by vessel from Cork to Quebec and subsequently by river to Kingston. In August, Robinson personally supervised the final stages of the scheme from the Lake Ontario shore to the relatively isolated and uninhabited area that had been selected for settlement which comprised six townships around the present site of Peterborough, extending fifty miles from east to west and twenty-five from north to south. The reason for selecting the area in the first place is not clear although Lieutenant-Governor Maitland gave a hint in 1824 when he expressed the hope that "the important line of communication between Richmond Landing on the Ottawa and Lake Simcoe could be settled".[9] This line lay more or less parallel to the north shore of Lake Ontario at a distance of thirty to forty miles from it and may have been thought to form a strategic route protected by distance from potential American attack.

The task of settling individual families of immigrants was personally undertaken by Robinson for a period of four months during which time he administered the new settlement. An item of interest is that the name Peterborough was first recorded in use by a surgeon accompanying the emigrants, in late 1825.[10]

Approximately ninety-three percent of the 2,024 Irish emigrants supervised by Peter Robinson settled in the six local townships of Asphodel, Douro, Emily, Ennismore, Otonabee and Smith.[11] The remainder of the emigrants settled in several scattered locations in Eastern Ontario. The total population of the townships is known for 1826 and the Irish appear to have formed a large proportion in most cases (Table I).[12]

The general distribution of Irish emigrant settlers may be observed in Figure 7.1. Numbers of settlers were unequally divided either side of the main water route, approximately two-fifths lying to the east of the Otonabee and the remainder to the west. The settlers were concentrated in two areas, one in Emily and Ennismore townships and the other in Douro township. These were separated by Smith township and the water bodies of Chemung Lake and the Otonabee, altogether comprising a distance of about ten miles. Very few settlers occupied land in Smith, and in the other townships of Asphodel and Otonabee a dispersed pattern of locations is apparent. Explanation of the general pattern of the distribution of Irish emigrants

TABLE I

Estimated Irish Emigrant Population by Township, 1826

Township	Township population	Irish Emigrants	Irish Emigrants as proportion of Total (percent by township)
Asphodel	253	185	73.5
Douro	273	265	98.2
Emily	837	563	67.5
Ennismore	290	315 (!)	100.0 (+)
Otonabee	368	210	57.1
Smith	339	145	42.8
Total	2,360	1,685	

in this area is problematical and will be returned to later in this paper.

The Peter Robinson emigration of 1825 provided a rapid influx of people into what was an unpopulated area. The population figures for Peterborough County townships, Table II, indicate the general distribution in the eighty years from 1826-1911. The delay in the settlement of northern parts of the county until after 1851 contrasts with the rapid rate of increase experienced in most southern townships. Of the six townships settled by the Irish emigrants of 1825, Otonabee's population increased at the greatest rate and Ennismore suffered from the lowest growth rate. Despite the concentration of Irish in Emily, Douro and Ennismore townships in 1825, a fact which temporarily boosted their population total, Otonabee township possessed the largest population after a period of twenty years had elapsed. The very size of the latter township may well have permitted a larger agricultural population. The relatively small proportion of Roman Catholic Irish settlers may have attracted others to Otonabee rather than to the "strongholds" of Emily, Douro and Ennismore.

The Northern Settlement on the Rocky Lands of Palaeozoic Outliers and Pre-Cambrian Shield

At the time that the last patents for Robinson's settlers were

TABLE II

Population by Township, Peterborough County, 1826-1911[14]

Township[15]	1826	1831	1841	1851	1861	1871	1881	1891	1901	1911
1 Asphodel	253	217	551	1678	2911	3247	1918	1866	1877	1661
2 Douro	273	321	858	1676	2519	2671	2864	2131	1871	1866
3 Emily	837	869	1851	2762	3923	3790	2876	2603	2304	2121
4 Ennismore	290	219	279	675	863	1104	1137	932	936	821
5 Otonabee	368	652	1931	3872	4261	3992	4013	3652	3456	3287
6 Smith	339	494	1349	2392	3795	3428	3301	3045	2944	2981
7 Dummer			868	1600	2105	1951	2149	2143	2039	1715
8 North Monaghan	276	708	2141	905	1281	1479	912	1021	957	1495
9 Anstruther				(with Dummer)	N.D.					
10 Belmont			115	248	689	1575	1738 (with Burleigh)	2548	2135	1824
11 Burleigh						721	1381	1520	687	352
12 Cavendish						521	787	94	155	262
13 Chandos						(with Burleigh)	(with Cavendish)		806	753
14 Galway					430	(with Cavendish)		N.D.	N.D.	338
15 Harvey			50	(with Smith)	360	670	1114	1155	1199	1027
16 Methuen				(with Belmont)			227	259	247	107

being issued in the early 1860s, when almost two generations
had elapsed in the settled area in the southern townships of
Peterborough County, plans for the assisted colonization of the
Pre-Cambrian Shield area of the province were in effect. In this
study the process of agricultural settlement will be described in
general terms in the area of Shield restricted to Harvey, Galway,
Cavendish and Anstruther townships in the north-western part
of present-day Peterborough County.

The Pre-Cambrian Shield extends across most of central and
eastern Ontario as a distinctive region both physically and
culturally. Reasons for its relative uniqueness in cultural terms
lie, as in any area, with the particular sequence of attitudes and
decisions evoked by the opportunities of the area. In this regard,
A.R.M. Lower has claimed that "no element in the present
Dominion of Canada is of greater significance than the so-called
Canadian Shield or Laurentian Barrier."[13]

The part of the Pre-Cambrian Shield occurring in Southern
Ontario is only a small part of its total extent. The position of the
southern edge of the Shield although imprecisely known in a
scientific sense until relatively recently had produced a distinct
response in those that settled in the valley of the St. Lawrence
River and its tributaries. The extremely resistant nature of the
igneous and metamorphic Pre-Cambrian rocks forming the
Shield hampered the course of streams and created falls and
rapids at numerous places. Access by water, the principal means
of movement before the last part of the nineteenth century, was
thus discouraged. Above Montreal, the Ottawa, the large left-
bank tributary of the St. Lawrence, joins the main stream. Both
rivers were, for a hundred or more miles above this point,
encumbered by rapids that greatly reduced their claim to being
major routeways. As a result the whole area above Montreal
became relatively isolated, Upper Canada suffered generally,
and the Shield area of eastern Ontario suffered particularly,
owing to the lack of agricultural opportunities and inaccessibil-
ity from the Great Lakes water route.

The Ottawa valley route was once used by French explorers,
missionaries and fur-traders to reach the Upper Great Lakes.
The route by-passed the Shield area and the latter may be
regarded as occupying the position of a backwater for most of
the French and early British period.

Official interest in the area appears to have commenced around 1819[16] when the British Government began a search for an alternative route to the St. Lawrence between the Ottawa River and Lake Huron. In that year, Lieutenant Catty traversed the Shield area from Lake Simcoe to the Ottawa River by the Madawaska River route. Seven years later, two separate military expeditions crossed the area, via the Madawaska, followed by another in 1827 further north. Reports of potential navigation routes were inconclusive. Two years later, Alexander Shirreff of Fitzroy Harbour surveyed the Ottawa River route to Georgian Bay and claimed it was superior to any rival cross-country route. He claimed in addition that the Pre-Cambrian Shield area was suitable for agriculture as it grew forests of hardwood trees, whereas in fact most of the area was devoid of soil beyond a thin layer of vegetable mould.

Sporadic interest in the area for navigation purposes continued until the 1850s, and other expeditions traversed the area including one, of three in 1837, led by David Thompson, the former Hudson's Bay Company surveyor. Very detailed observations and maps were made on this survey, on a route via the Madawaska River, although they were virtually ignored by other surveyors in subsequent decades.[17]

The gradual process of extending township surveys away from the main lake and river-front resulted in the present area of northern Peterborough County being surveyed first in the 1820s. Andrew Miller surveyed Harvey in 1823 and commented unfavourably upon its potential for cultivation. In 1827, John Huston submitted reports on the four townships of Harvey, Galway, Cavendish and Anstruther, yet reported little land that was fit for settlement. Despite this early pessimism, subsequent surveys were not only made but resulted in some doubt about the pessimism with regard to agriculture in the area. Apart from Shirreff's aforementioned recommendation, Thompson himself reported in 1837 that considerable areas in the Muskoka region of the Shield were fit for cultivation.

Guillet notes that G.B. Hall was one of the most prominent early settlers of the southern Harvey township. He constructed a dam and grist and saw mill in the 1830s at Hall's Bridge or Buckhorn, as it is now called, on the rapids that existed there. The dam was enlarged in 1836 when the initial steps for raising lake levels and improving water navigation in the Kawartha Lakes were taken.[18]

Apart from Hall, several gentlemen settlers were attracted, allegedly by the scenery and the game, to the southwest corner of Harvey township in 1832, near Pigeon and Sandy Lake.[19] In his reminiscences, Samuel Strickland wrote:

> The spot chosen by them was one of great natural beauty, but it possessed no other advantages except an abundance of game, which was no small inducement to them. They spent several thousand pounds in building fancy log houses and making large clearings which they had neither the ability nor the industry to cultivate. But even if they had possessed sufficient perseverence, their great distance from markets, bad roads, want of knowledge of cropping after they had cleared the land, lack of bridges, and poor soil would have been a great drawback to the chance of effecting a prosperous settlement.[20]

All the settlers described left the area after a few years, either penniless or to better farms or occupations more suited to their actual abilities.

Settlement in the Middle to Late Nineteenth Century

By the 1850s pressure of settlement on the older townships and diversion of emigrants, as a result, to the United States acted as a spur to the Legislative Assembly to open more land for agricultural settlement. This they proceeded to do in the 1850s despite an eloquent and authoritative recommendation in 1853 by surveyor J.W. Bridgland who reported on the Muskoka area of the Shield and hoped that his report provided

> a knowledge of what the country really is, and a consequent safeguard, against incurring future expenses in the subdivision of a country into Townships, and farm lots, which is entirely unfitted, as a whole, for agricultural purposes.[21]

Encouragement for settlement of the Shield came from other sources however, both within the Crown Lands Department of the provincial Government and among the lumbermen. Apart from increasing the permanent population of the province, further agricultural settlement in the Ottawa-Huron tract, as the Shield area was called, would provide a local source of provisions for the lumber industry.

The provincial Legislature passed the Public Lands Act in 1853 which permitted free grants of one hundred acres to be made to actual settlers on, or near to, colonization roads which were to be constructed. A colonization fund also was set up by the Act, of which $30,000 was for roads and land-grants in Canada West. The colonization roads were created in the fifteen years preceding Confederation in 1867, when 481 miles were completed in the Ottawa-Huron Tract.[22] In the study area, the Buckhorn Road was constructed as part of this communication network intended to link Hall's Bridge in the south by a direct route to the land belonging to the Canada Land and Emigration Company in present-day Haliburton County, fifty miles to the north.[23] The Buckhorn Road was surveyed in 1863 with construction commencing in 1865. It was one of the last colonization roads to be built and was parallel to other earlier roads both to the east, the Burleigh and Hastings Roads, and to the west, the Bobcaygeon Road. Of the projected road length of fifty-six miles only thirty-four were in fact constructed by 1866 extending to the Monck Road, an east to west route, and stopping short of the Company land. The failure of the road to reach this area and the availability of free Crown Land nearby resulted in the demise of this Company by the mid-1870s.

Owing to the failure of permanent agricultural settlement, relatively little change has occurred in the century since the creation of the colonization roads. The Buckhorn Road and its associated settlement features represents a fossilized landscape which can be inspected in order to gain a first-hand glimpse of previous conditions. At its southern end, two miles north of Buckhorn, the road ascends a flat-topped hill formed by an outlier of Palaeozoic limestone strata. In the vicinity of Flynn's Turn the appearance of farming landscape presents a stark contrast to the largely forested rolling terrain of the surrounding Shield. Soils on the limestone are thin but apparently sufficient to have supported farming activities up to the recent past. A good view of the Shield from the outlier is obtained north of the junction at Flynn's Turn. The landscape in the immediate vicinity resembles that of the settled area in southern Peterborough County with cleared fields, rail fences and occasional farm buildings, the latter displaying a variety of construction materials including cut blocks of local limestone. The straight course of the Buckhorn Road on the limestone outlier changes dramatically to the tortuous route further north. Settlement is less evident and the roadside landscape of forest bears no sign of clearance for large distances. The undulating winding course of the present highway is mute testimony to the problems of constructing a road across the Shield with nineteenth century techniques. Travel on colonization roads such as this appears to have been difficult at best, as the following description relating to the neighbouring Bobcaygeon Road testifies:

> . . . The railway bringing us to Lindsay forty miles the first day then by steamer the next day twenty miles to Bobcaygeon, the remaining forty I can scarcely describe for if any road was made purposely to upset the passengers, the Bobcaygeon must be the one.[24]

The difficulties of access even along the road itself aggravated the problem of settlement of the Shield. The route of the colonization road did not deliberately link areas of agricultural potential and it was by chance that fertile soils lay close to the road. Settlement did not spread over the northern townships in a uniform line from the older area partly because the roads provided relatively deep penetration into the Shield and planned settlement along these communication arteries did not materialize on any but a discontinuous basis.[25]

Agricultural settlement in the area was accomplished only by creating routes, often little more than trails, from the main colonization road into the patches of usable land. This did little to improve accessibility of the Shield farms to the markets of Southern Ontario. This isolating factor may have made bush farms largely dependent upon local markets, a dependency which was greatest when lumbering was at its height in the last decades of the nineteenth century. With the decline of lumbering, the farms proved uneconomical and fell into decay.[26]

The population of the northern townships of Peterborough

County is seen to have increased slowly during the period up to the first decade of the present century after which a decline became apparent (Table II). The slow increase in population of these townships is reflected in data of agricultural activity, the acres of occupied farmland, for example, having increased from approximately 2,000 in 1841 to 45,300 acres in 1881. The slow growth was caused partly by the low potential of the area for agriculture and in addition by the alternative outlet for agricultural settlement found in the plains of both the western United States and Canada. The attraction of these areas increased as the nineteenth century drew to a close, reinforced by the decline in lumbering and mining locally.

The agricultural settlement of the Shield in Peterborough County involved relatively few individuals over a period of fifty years during which time essentially local markets for produce emerged and subsequently declined. The estimation of place utility on the part of settlers in this area appears to have been influenced by market access and land quality considerations primarily, the latter variable emphasized because of the extremely infertile character of most of the Shield. Both influences appear to have had a greater prominence in the settlement decision than in the area further south, partly because of the later date when more information was available and greater structure existed in the production and marketing of agricultural produce.

The level of analysis of the motives of settlers has been quite different for the Shield area than for the settlement in 1825. This is partly because of the lack of information of individual settlement and of the environmental characteristics of land quality. The settlement contrast in the land close to the margin of the Shield is great both in terms of the existing landscape and from the point of view of the influences underlying the agricultural settlement of these areas by individuals.

Assessment of Place Utility by Irish Emigrants of 1825

The distribution of Irish emigrants in the Peterborough County area appears to have been scattered almost randomly over six contiguous townships. The reasons for this distribution may be understood more perfectly if the assessment of place utility by the emigrants is explained in terms of various general factors.

The question ''What was the place utility of the locations occupied by the Irish?'' will be addressed by considering in turn the influences that were previously mentioned as traditionally having importance in the assessment of place utility. These are the compulsory nature of official control, the opportunity of employment, the accessibility factor with regard to society in all its aspects, and finally the character of the environment in general.

1) The Influence of Official Control on Place Utility.
The Irish emigrants appear to have been greatly influenced by this factor and so great may its influence have been that the assessment of local place utility may not have been possible for the majority.

The government of Upper Canada appears to have directed the 1825 emigrants to the Newcastle District in the area of present-day Peterborough because population was deemed desirable in this essentially remote area. A protected land route between Lake Simcoe and the Ottawa River was envisaged to offer an alternative to the exposed lakeshore route along Lake Ontario. No specific route was developed or surveyed and the marked non-linearity of the Irish locations offers no clue to its course. Nevertheless the routeway may have formed the principal reason for the Irish presence in 1825.

At the more detailed level of the township and individual lot, better choice of location may have been offered to the emigrants. Locations appear to have been allocated by drawing lots[27], and choice was only subsequently possible by exchange with others for their locations.[28] No prior appraisal of available free land or inspection of land quality seems to have been possible.

The proportion of land already granted or reserved before the arrival of the Irish varied among the six townships from twenty-eight per cent in Ennismore (the Crown and Clergy Reserves only) to two-thirds of the lots in Asphodel, with the average of 44.7 per cent of lots unavailable. The Irish were occupying townships already partly claimed although choice was still possible in late 1825.

2) The Influence of Opportunity for Employment on Place Utility.

This may have had a relatively weak influence on place utility assessment owing to the assumption that self-sufficient agriculture, plus government subsidy for several years, would provide a livelihood. In Upper Canada as with most areas of the New World in the early nineteenth century this assumption rendered this factor relatively unimportant in place utility assessment of the majority of emigrants.

Peter Robinson was ordered to select only farmers and their families for the emigration and even the fact that he permitted other occupations to join, approximately one quarter of the total, did not alter the general expectations of the emigrants with regard to source of livelihood.[29]

3) The Influence of Accessibility to Social and Economic Functions.

The general pattern of settlement suggests a division in the Irish settlement between the western location in Emily and Ennismore, and the eastern ones in Douro, Otonabee and Asphodel. The two clusters of settlements appear to be separated by formidable barriers including the Otonabee River and Chemung Lake and the locations may have reflected the availability of extensive contiguous free land in both these areas with little previous settlement in either.

In Emily and Ennismore apart from the scatter of reserves which were naturally unsettled, land alienated and settled prior to the Irish emigration was in the southern and western part of the former township.[30] The Irish appear to have occupied the remaining free land in north-eastern Emily and Ennismore much of which is a peninsula jutting between Pigeon, Buckhorn and Chemung Lakes. Relatively few Irish settlers chose or were obliged to settle in the southern occupied part of Emily. The settlers in this area were Ulstermen and may not have been mutually acceptable neighbours to the Robinson emigrants.

To the east the settlement and land claims before November, 1825, had taken up a great deal of the land bordering the Otonabee River, Rice Lake, and its outflow the Trent. The Irish occupied, possibly as a direct result, lands away from the waterway or to the north of the previous settled limit. In areas east and west of the Otonabee, the Irish appeared to move onto lands further north than previously granted or settled. In central Otonabee and Asphodel considerable inter-mingling with other settlers appears to have been the pattern of location. In northern Otonabee and southern Douro townships however, as in Emily and Ennismore to the west, a virtually uniform spread of Robinson Irish settlers closely occupied the area.

This pattern of settlement suggests that the availability of land may have merely reinforced the desire for ready access to others of Irish background. To this day Irish communities exist in these two areas and suggest that a similar spirit influenced initial settlement. The two principal centres of concentration possess further characteristics in terms of the social ties of individual emigrants that may be significant in explaining settlement location.

Just over half of the emigrant families came from only thirteen villages in Ireland. Many of these appear to have settled close together. Of twenty-four families from Brigown, thirteen went to Douro Township to make up almost one third of the total settlers there. Nine families from Listowel located in Ennismore to form one-fifth of the settlers in that township. A quarter of the settlers in Emily township came from only two villages, Kilworth and Mallow, both of which places sent over half their emigrant families to the township. These concentrations of Irish from the same village involved one-sixth of the total 252 families and may represent the most obvious examples of the influence of the desire for close access to familiar individuals in settlement. Some evidence appears to exist for concentration of settlers by common emigration vessel and this too may have provided a basis of acquaintance which was an important consideration in terms of accessibility of neighbours.[31]

In terms of access to economic functions the evidence suggests that little importance was placed on the route of principal communications or the sites of mills or other central functions. The previously referred-to remoteness of many of the Irish locations suggests little knowledge or concern on the part of the authorities or the emigrants, on this score.

4) The Influence of the Environment on Place Utility.
Of the characteristics of the physical and cultural environment

which the Irish emigrants occupied in 1825 several may have been particularly important in influencing place utility. The quality of the land for agriculture was perhaps the paramount physical environmental consideration. Relatively little evidence supports the suggestion that the Irish emigrants consciously sought out good land even if they were able to recognize it. Rather it appears that they may have collectively trusted Peter Robinson and the authorities to locate them in an area with some agricultural potential. The distribution of loam or sand-loam soils which possess good qualities for agriculture is quite extensive, covering about fifty-five per cent of the area. The Irish settlers occupied such land in a large proportion of instances.

Cultural environmental characteristics that may have influenced place utility were perhaps those of language, religion and social familiarity. In each of these cases, the nature of the emigration ensured the individual Irish emigrant of the preservation of much of his familiar home environment. Once again it may be safe to assume that the majority of emigrants relied on the authorities to provide a cultural environment satisfactory to them.

In summary, the assessment of place utility by Irish emigrants of 1825 in the Peterborough area appears to have been generally influenced by official control of settlement which included the choice of the area and specific lots of land to be occupied as well as the general social environment of the area. Individual choice appears to have been possible only to a limited extent in agricultural settlement, and may have resulted in settlers from certain villages in Ireland exchanging lots to be in the same areas. A few Irish emigrants rejected settlement immediately and left for other areas.

The Regional Catalyst in Retrospect

The emigration of Irish people to the Peterborough area in 1825 ended the period of isolation and may have been the single most important event in the settlement of the area. From it grew the town of Peterborough and an agricultural hinterland extending over a large area. The degree of success enjoyed by individuals in the emigration cannot be easily described but in general terms the success may be measured in regard to the Irish as a group, the British government and the population of the Peterborough area.

The Irish settlers appear to have clearly benefitted from the emigration both in terms of the actual gifts of nourishment for eighteen months[32] and the tools, livestock, seed and other items useful in settlement, and in addition, in terms of the opportunity to improve their lives. Several writers have judged the emigration most successful from the social or philanthropic point of view. Local historians have understandably expressed this view[33] and have generally received support of a more objective kind from writers such as Pammett, Cowan and Gates.[34] The Irish settlers of 1825 remained in the area and Gates suggests that all settlers to be issued land received their full title, the majority in the first decade after settlement, but a few as late as 1862. Relatively few persons left the area for other parts of North America which suggests a high place utility assessment persisted.[35] Later Irish emigrants in the 1840s did not settle on the land and occupied poorer areas of towns soon after arriving in the province. They may have rejected agricultural settlement deliberately as a way of life although they were apparently less skilled and poorer than the emigrants of 1825.[36]

The question of cost per immigrant to the British Government was one which was unsatisfactorily answered in the period following the settlement. Although Robinson claimed in 1827 that a family of five could be settled in Upper Canada for £60 or approximately £12 a head, he had quite incorrectly, as Gates pointed out, based calculations of wealth on value of possessions, ignoring debts and the actual availability of accumulated wealth as currency.[37] Gates claimed that in 1846 the assessed valuation of holdings settled by Robinson immigrants was scarcely greater than the cost of the emigration twenty-one years earlier, suggesting it was a great expense and relatively unsuccessful in strict economic terms. The government acted to change the basis on which land was alienated in Upper Canada, ending the system of free grants in 1826 only a few months after Robinson's emigration, and henceforth land was sold to individuals by auction.

In assessing its overall value, Pammett attributed to the Robinson settlement the achievement of rapidly opening up the

whole area around the present city of Peterborough and providing it with

> . . . . an impetus which is still felt, in progress and mutual aid
> and the advancement of the community. No visitor to the
> prosperous and well-cultivated townships of Otonabee,
> Douro, Smith, Asphodel, Emily and Ennismore can have any
> doubts as to the benefits of the movement from Ireland to
> Canada in 1825, both for the Irish themselves and for the
> Peterborough district.[38]

Conclusion

The settlement process in Peterborough County proceeded over
a period of fifty or more years after 1820. Throughout this
period a general similarity characterized the settlers and the
organization of settlement yet the marked differences in physical environment within the county produced sharply contrasting
settlement landscapes. The glacial drift-covered southern land
was extensively occupied and converted for agriculture, the
most dramatic event in this process being perhaps the settlement
of the Irish emigrants in 1825. The northern part of the county
was penetrated by several routes, or colonization roads, in the
1850s and 1860s and only subsequently and quite incompletely
did settlers trickle into the area to establish farms on whatever
soil they could find. A process of abandonment of farming
quickly followed settlement in much of the latter area and
accentuated the contrast between Shield and drift-covered
areas.

Notes on Primary Sources

City of Peterborough Public Library (also in Provincial Archives of Ontario and Public Archives of Canada), Manuscript
volume on Robinson emigrants of 1825 listed by township,
microfilm Reel no. 2, vol. 3.

Trent University, Bata Library, Assessment Rolls of Emily,
Ennismore, Smith, Douro, Otonabee and Asphodel townships,
for 1826, 1827 and 1828, microfilm.

Notes

¹Julian Wolpert, "Behavioural Aspects of the Decision to Migrate", *Papers and Proceedings, Regional Science Association*, Vol. 15, 1965, p. 161.

²C.C. Roseman, "Migration as a Spatial and Temporal Process", *Annals*, Association of American Geographers, Vol. 61, No. 3, 1971, p. 592.

³Roseman, "Migration as a Spatial and Temporal Process", p. 594, and A.G. Brunger, "A Spatial Analysis of Individual Settlement in Southern London District, Upper Canada, 1800-1836", unpublished Ph.D. thesis, University of Western Ontario, 1973, p. 18.

⁴L.J. Chapman and D.F. Putnam, *The Physiography of Southern Ontario*, 2nd ed. (Toronto, 1966), p. 313.

⁵J.A. Edmison (ed.), *Through the Years in Douro* (Peterborough, 1967), pp. 6, 8.

⁶Edmison, *op. cit.*, p. 9, and T.W. Poole, *The Early Settlement of Peterborough County* (Peterborough, 1867), pp. 123-167 (reprinted 1967).

⁷Edmison, *Through the Years . . . op. cit.*, p. 9.

⁸H.T. Pammett, "Assisted Irish Emigration to Upper Canada under Peter Robinson in 1825, including the City of Peterborough and Surrounding Townships", unpublished M.A. thesis, Queen's University, 1934, and "Assisted Emigration from Ireland to Upper Canada under Peter Robinson in 1825", *Ontario History*, vol. 31 (1936), pp. 178-214.

⁹H.I. Cowan, *British Emigration to British North America*, rev. ed., (Toronto, 1961), pp. 74-84.

¹⁰Pammett, "Assisted Emigration from Ireland . . . ," *op. cit.*, pp. 193, 201.

¹¹The Robinson Papers, show that 1685 Irish people settled in these six townships. Pammett states that 1878 persons were settled in the Newcastle District around Scott's Plains, *op. cit.*, 1936, p. 195. Emily township is in Victoria rather than Peterborough County.

¹²*Journals, House of Assembly, Upper Canada*, 1826; Appendix, Census of Upper Canada, 1825.

¹³A.R.M. Lower, "The Assault on the Laurentian Barrier, 1850-1870", *Canadian Historical Review*, Vol. x (1929), p. 294.

¹⁴The population data are derived from the Appendices of the *Journals of the Legislative Assembly* for the years 1826-1841, and from the *Census of Canada* for the period 1851-1911. Data for the year 1850 from the Appendices and for 1851 from the census have been compared and tend to differ such that the accuracy of one or other, or both, sources is called into question. Emily township is included because many Irish located there in 1825.

[15]The townships are arranged such that the first six are those settled by Irish emigrants in 1825. The first eight are all in the southern part of the county. The remaining eight are all in the northern part of Peterborough county and are totally or partially in the Pre-Cambrian Shield.

[16]F.B. Murray, *Muskoka and Haliburton, 1615-1875* (Toronto, 1963), p. xiv.

[17]*Ibid.*, p. iii.

[18]E.C. Guillet, *The Valley of the Trent* (Toronto: Champlain Society, 1957), p. 214.

[19]M.J. Wagner, "Gentry Perception and Land Utilization in the Peterborough-Kawartha Lakes Region, 1818-1851", unpublished M.A. thesis, University of Toronto, 1968, pp. 30-31.

[20]Samuel Strickland, *Twenty-Seven Years in Canada West*, Vol. 1 (London, 1853), pp. 135-136, quoted in Wagner, *op. cit.*, p. 31.

[21]Murray, *op. cit.*, p. 156, from J.W. Bridgland's "Report . . . of exploring lines from the Eldon Portage to the Mouth of the River Muskoka," Toronto, January 31, 1853.

[22]G.W. Spragge, "Colonization Roads in Canada West, 1850-1867", *Ontario History*, Vol. XLIX (1957), p. 17.

[23]Poole, *The Early Settlement of Peterborough County*, pp. 192, 205.

[24]Guillet, *The Valley of the Trent* (1957), p. 80, letter from A. Parsonage, Dysart, February 29, 1864.

[25]J.H.B. Richards, "Land-use and Settlement Patterns on the Shield in Southern Ontario", unpublished Ph.D. thesis University of Toronto, 1954, and "Agricultural Patterns in the Precambrian Area of Southern Ontario", *The Canadian Geographer*, Vol. I, no. 5 (1955), p. 65.

[26]About five miles north of Flynn's Turn, the Buckhorn Road passes through the aptly-named hamlet of Rockcroft, comprising a handful of farms astride the route. Scattered farms are visible along the route with decreasing frequency as the road proceeds northward.

[27]Pammett, "Assisted Emigration from Ireland . . ." *op. cit.*, p. 195.

[28]Edmison, *op. cit.*, p. 17

[29]Pammett, *op. cit.*, p. 182.

[30]Public Archives of Ontario, Index of Land Patents by Township.

[31]G.R. Ferguson, "The Peter Robinson Emigration of 1825 and Some Factors Influencing the Location of Settlers", unpublished B.Sc. thesis, Trent University, 1972, pp. 59, 66-72.

[32]Pammett, "Assisted Emigration from Ireland . . . ," *op. cit.*, p. 207.

[33]Edmison, *op. cit.*, p. 19, Poole, *op. cit.*, p. 12.

[34]Pammett (1936), *op. cit.*, pp. 213-14; Cowan, *British Emigration to North America*, p. 82, and L.F. Gates, *Land Policies in Upper Canada* (Toronto, 1968), p. 97.

35Evidence of the persistent Irish occupance of the area is seen in the collection of essays and documents, *Through the Years in Douro*, edited by J.M. Edmison. See also John Mannion, *Irish Settlements in Eastern Canada* (University of Toronto Press, 1974); H.T. Pammett, *Lilies and Shamrocks* (Toronto, 1974).

36Kenneth Duncan, ''Irish Famine Immigration and the Social Structure of Canada West'', *Canadian Review of Sociology and Anthropology*, Vol. 2 (1965), p. 24.

37Gates, *Land Policies in Upper Canada*, p. 97.

38Pammett, ''Assisted Emigration from Ireland . . . ,'' *op. cit.*, pp. 213-214.

8. THE CANADA COMPANY AND LAND SETTLEMENT AS RESOURCE DEVELOPMENT IN THE GUELPH BLOCK

James M. Cameron

This paper is a brief examination of a particular approach to land settlement, an approach illustrated by the activities of the Canada Company, a public stock company formed in the early nineteenth century. It focuses on the Company's approach to resource development and its activities in the Guelph settlement, and particularly the town of Guelph. The period under examination begins in 1827 with the founding of Guelph by John Galt, the first Superintendent of the Company, and ends in 1851 with the removal of the Canada Company agency from Guelph to Toronto, after which, with the coming of the railways, a new era began in the development of the area.

Some comment should be made here regarding the scene and set of circumstances in Upper Canada prior to 1825 regarding land settlement. Beginning in the late eighteenth century, the British Government had supported and attempted a number of approaches to the settlement of lands in Upper Canada. The "leader and associates" system of land grants was begun in 1792 and involved making a large grant to an individual who promised to bring in settlers to occupy the lands granted.[1] This system was generally not successful, either as a result of speculation or mismanagement and was abandoned although there were examples of similar arrangements after the end of the Simcoe era. The British Government later undertook various schemes aimed at assisting or subsidizing particular groups to leave the British Isles and settle in the colonies (for example, Scottish settlers in the Rideau District between 1815 and 1821, and Irish settlers around Peterborough in 1825), but after an extensive review of the schemes by Parliamentary Committees in 1826 and 1827, it was decided that they had cost too much to be repeated.[2]

After about 1825 the primary source of settlers for Upper Canada was the unassisted immigration of private individuals. By this time a growing number of people from every walk of life were planning to emigrate from the British Isles not because they were destitute, but because they felt themselves to be steadily slipping, unable to maintain, let alone improve, their present level of living. By the early 1820s, it was becoming evident that basic changes would have to be made in land policies if Upper Canada was to be prepared to receive a growing immigrant population. Past regulations and practices had proved to be hopelessly inadequate and unsatisfactory as they had tried to accomplish nearly every imaginable purpose except that of encouraging compact and effective settlement.[3] From available figures it would appear that less than a tenth of the land granted by the government prior to 1825 had been even occupied by settlers, much less cultivated.[4] It was within this setting that the Canada Company emerged. One of the originators of the idea for a land company to acquire the unalienated lands in Upper Canada was John Galt, a Scottish novelist. Galt had connections with London investors, and in a short time, he had a scheme worked out which formed the basis of an agreement made late in 1824 between Lord Bathurst, Secretary of State for War and the Colonies, and the financial subscribers. It was originally planned that the Company would receive all of the remaining Crown Reserves in the surveyed townships of Upper Canada, and half of the Clergy Reserves, as of March 1st, 1824. However, as a result of a vocal lobby by the Clergy group under the leadership of John Strachan, the Clergy reserves were withdrawn from the transaction, and in their place the Company was to receive a block of one million acres of land (later increased to 1,100,000 acres to allow for swamps and bad land) in the London and Western districts. This block of land became known as the Huron Tract. (See Figure 1.1). In the final terms, the Company was to pay a total of £348,680 7s 2d sterling over a period of sixteen years (1827-1843), for a total of 2,484,413 acres.[5] The final average cost for the land obtained was 2s 10d per acre. The management of the Company was to be by a Court of Directors resident in London with a commission of two or more persons resident in Upper Canada to manage the affairs there.

Conditions Necessary for Land Development

Before an interpretation can be made of the Canada Company's approach to resource development, a basic framework for analysis must be presented. The process of land settlement in a previously unsettled area is a complex one. It involves a considerable number of conditions in the correct proportions before the settlement will be undertaken, and then a number of other conditions if the settlement is to succeed. A brief framework of the factors involved in resource development by a land settlement scheme, and in particular, the conditions favourable to such a scheme are presented here.

1) Incentives

Before a land settlement scheme can become a reality, there must be incentives present. The situation must be such that there is a feeling of optimism and that opportunities are favourable enough to attract the people who will provide the labour and the capital (looking for a profit) which will bring together the people and the land resource. The optimism and the opportunities must also enable the organization factor (management) to envisage success for the scheme as well as to see how the opportunities which are present can be brought together in a workable manner.

2) Natural Resources and Technology

The chief natural resource under consideration is that of land. However, land regarded with its economic implications implies not mere land alone, but the climate, topography, soil, vegetation cover, water, location and access to markets with which it is associated. Together these help determine what the land is best for, thus what production is possible. With regard to pioneer land settlement in the period under consideration, it is clear that land must be available in sufficient quantity and at a low enough price if it is to be developed. Finally, the land resource must be able to be developed with the current technology if the land settlement scheme is to succeed.

3) People (Labour)

People are of primary importance to a land development scheme, providing labour, socio-cultural enrichment, and individual initiative. Pioneer agriculture is labour demanding. The more primitive the state of technology, the higher is the proportion of labour to capital. The labour source may be either immigration or migration from areas within the country under examination. The quality of the people (immigrants or migrants) is also significant. They must be willing to work and live under pioneer conditions, they must be resourceful and hardworking, and it is preferable that they bring with them some relevant skills, either in trades or farming. The rate of assimilation of the new settlers into the settlement scheme as well as the length of time before the new settlers become part of the productive process is also critical. Finally, under the heading of people, mention must be made of the role of personalities in a land settlement scheme—a fact which acknowledges the importance of individual settlers and managers whose leadership and abilities set them above the group.

4) Capital

Capital, a factor of production, also plays an essential role in a land settlement scheme. Capital formation means that society does not apply all of its current production actions to the needs and desires of present consumption, but instead directs part of it to the making of capital goods, such as tools, transport, plant and equipment. Thus, delaying consumption means reducing consumption now (reduced income) in hopes for a greater income later. It should be noted that a land settlement scheme will not develop a strong capital base unless the individuals that make up the scheme do some saving of their own, and can see for themselves the necessity of capital formation. The sources of capital are both external and internal, and from private sources as well as government, with the government usually providing the social overhead capital (infrastructure) while the private sector's interest lies in providing the production facilities, for example, cleared farms, mills, etc. The capital provided in the form of credit by the directors of a land settlement scheme brings together the factors of land and labour. With regard to capital and the terms of its provision, the rate of interest is a very important price in the economic system as well as being related to incentives both to the settler and to investors.

5) Markets

Markets also play a vital role in a land settlement scheme. Markets determine the prices for and quantities of the agricultural products being produced. With steady markets and adequate prices, most settlers are assured of a return for their labour, and capital is assured a return on its investment. The accessibility of the producers to markets and the efficiency of the marketing process are both important. Also, an initial problem faced by a land development scheme is heavy reliance on one or two exports, thus making the scheme more vulnerable to adverse physical and economic changes.

6) Infrastructure

Infrastructure, or social overhead capital, involves the facilities which are required for production and distribution (for example, transportation, plant and equipment) and social facilities (for example, education, health). Infrastructure is of considerable importance in a land settlement scheme in order to decrease the time period between the initiation of the scheme and the emergence of a viable, productive community. For example, the provision of initial transportation facilities (in this case roads) prior to the settlement of the land, acts as a considerable stimulus to settlement because the economic costs involved are not borne directly by the early settlers struggling for survival and establishment, but are borne by the land development company or the government. By providing these facilities early, the settlement can focus its attention on producing for the market. In a developing area, the infrastructure initially may not have enough work to do, or enough demand for its services to justify its introduction at an early date. It can only be justified as an encouragement and catalyst for development.

7) Institutional Arrangements

Institutional arrangements (organization) play a critical role in a land settlement scheme. It is not enough simply to say that development is a function of natural resources, technology, people, capital, markets, and infrastructure. It is institutional arrangements (organization) which combine these factors in the right proportions and in so doing set the tone and structure of the settlement scheme. Institutional arrangements involve such things as the roles of, and division of responsibilities between, government and private sectors; social facilities in the community; the part played by urban units in the land settlement scheme; the information channels in operation; and finally, the type of farm organization and size.

8) Transformation

Transformation (diversification) means a change in the structure, function, and resource allocation of the scheme as part of the process of economic development.[6] Initially, the natural resources contribute directly to meeting the settlers' demands for food, fuel, etc. However, as the population grows and the markets widen, these same natural resources become the base for a more complex economic organization with ever increasing specialization of labour, and larger accumulations of capital both from external and internal sources.[7] Thus, diversification of production takes the place of the single commodity, export-based community. The urban units gradually become independent forces rather than being completely dependent on agriculture.[8] What are the criteria for judging success of a development scheme? "Success" involves several levels. Success for the settler, either as an individual or as a family unit, is measured in terms of income as well as in the achievement of the non-economic objectives of security and satisfaction with his position and his progress in the settlement. Success for the land development company, however, is as critical to the scheme as success for the settler, though based more on the criterion of rates of return on investment both in the short and long run. Success can also be examined for other kinds of investors (both family and firm) who are attracted to the development scheme to engage in commerce, manufacturing and finance. Here again success is measured both in economic (returns on investment) and non-economic terms.

There are several other points of view for examining the success of a development scheme. There is the success as measured by the permanence and continuity of the settlement over time. There is the success as measured by the achievement or failure of the government's objectives which may be economic, military or social in nature. Finally, there is the success as measured by changes in the economic structure within the scheme, rising to higher levels of development as described previously under the heading of transformation.

A land settlement undertaking is complex and usually precarious, as detailed above. The foregoing discussion has prepared a framework for the examination of a particular land settlement scheme as an approach to resource development.

Interpretation of the Canada Company's Approach to Resource Development

The Canada Company was a large scale private land development company which purchased large areas of land in Upper Canada from the British Government with the object of reselling this land to settlers and thereby making a profit. Although the Company's operations and influence were widespread throughout the province, this brief analysis will only examine the Guelph settlement and focus on the factors of capital, infrastructure, and transformation.

When Upper Canada was first settled, the Niagara District was surveyed without reserving one-seventh for the Crown, and when the Crown Reserves were created, the Crown's proportion of land was set aside in Blocks in the unsurveyed or partially surveyed townships. Guelph township in the District of Gore was such a Block. When Guelph was founded by John Galt in April, 1827, the surrounding townships had been alienated from the Crown to ownership by individuals for some period of time, but in most, little actual settlement had taken place.

1) Capital
Perhaps the most significant point concerning the Canada Com-

pany is the fact that it was an agent of initial capital introduction prior to local capital accumulation. Quoting Easterbrook and Aitken who comment on the period of the 1830s, "the process of assimilating immigrants into the productive organization of the colony was essentially, from the economic point of view, a process of investment".[9] The Company's payments to government and expenditures on improvements contributed greatly to the growth of the provincial economy both by increasing the flow of money and by building the basic physical infrastructure for transportation and production. The Company also assisted in this process of capital accumulation by means of its deferred payment purchase plan and leasing with option to purchase, both of which provided credit to immigrants until they were able to acquire sufficient capital (in the form of cleared land, stock, and buildings) to continue on their own and repay the Company out of current production.[10] The buoyant effect of the early expenditures of the Company in the Guelph settlement is very noticeable, as well as the slump in the period 1828-1830 when the Company's interest waned in the Guelph settlement.

It is important to note here that, particularly in the early years, the progress and prosperity of the town and surrounding township were almost inseparable. The Company brought in a number of workmen and mechanics, including a blacksmith, shoemaker, baker, wagon-maker, and carpenter. The early immigrants were also hired to work on Company projects and in June, 1827, there were between forty and fifty men working as labourers for the Company. A number of groups of settlers, mainly Scots, arrived in the summer of 1827 with one group settling in the Scotch Block (along what is now the Elora Road) while another group settled in the Paisley Block to the west of the new town. In 1827 a large number of lots, both farm and town, were taken up. The town in this period was used as a stopping-off place for settlers on their way to taking up land. The spring of 1828 opened rather ominously with differences arising between Galt and the Directors over the scale of the Company's expenditures in the Guelph settlement. These expenditures were thus curtailed, and as a result, nearly all the skilled workmen left, with only those who intended to become permanent settlers remaining. Galt left finally for England in the spring of 1829. The Guelph settlement came to a standstill, with the Company unwilling to continue its expenditures. Also, there was an absence of people, in both town and country, with sufficient capital to carry on business. Up to this period, nearly all the settlers were emigrants direct from Britain with little means or experience to help them. Provisions were scarce, and there was hardly any cash to purchase what little was offered for sale. The years 1829-1830 were indeed dismal throughout the Guelph Block.[11] See Figure 8.1.

8.1   The Guelph settlement, about 1830. Foreground: Allen's Bridge and The Priory (original Canada Co. headquarters); middle ground: stone schoolhouse (fenced) and immigrant reception building (with flag). From *Fraser's Magazine*.

The year 1832 was the turning point in the early development of Guelph and area. Immigration to Canada increased considerably and the Company was quick to take advantage of this by stepping up their publicity campaign in Britain. The Company's agent, recently appointed at Quebec, had been a resident in Guelph, and was acquainted with the customs of the country as well as the particular advantages of Guelph and the opportunities there. In 1832 a large influx of settlers arrived primarily from England, many of whom were men of some capital and education. Many of these new settlers purchased partially cleared farms in Guelph Township from old settlers, or they bought wild land from the Company. Thus, with this influx of capital, a local market was created for produce, new stores and taverns appeared, and Guelph was on its feet permanently. According to the Directors Report for 1831, Guelph contained a gristmill, a sawmill, a distillery in full operation, and one about to be put into operation, a tannery under construction, a brewery, five inns, four merchant shops and a druggist, four blacksmith shops, and three churches either built or in the process of being built.[12] The following is from a Canada Company advertisement published in the *Montreal Gazette* of May 7, 1832, which comments on the Guelph settlement:

> From the class of emigrants that have lately gone there, and from the conveniences afforded in a settlement of some standing, it will be found a desirous residence for persons of moderate capital.[13]

The stage had been set for future development.

Some comment should be made here regarding the Company's investment in the Guelph settlement and the rate of return it obtained on this investment. The total investment of the Company in the Guelph settlement between 1827 and 1851 was approximately £20,000 while its revenue (sales and leases) in the same period was nearly £40,000. However, it should be noted that nearly all of the capital was invested prior to 1830, while the return on investment in the form of revenue was spread over the entire period to 1851. In order to determine more accurately whether or not the Company made a profit on its investment, the value of its investments and revenues was calculated with interest compounded at six per cent per annum to the year 1851. An interest rate of six per cent was used because this was the rate of interest which was general in the colony during this period. As a result of these calculations it appears that the Company's rate of return over the period 1827-1851 in the Guelph settlement was approximately eleven per cent per annum on its investment which was indeed favourable for the Company. It should be emphasized here, however, that while in the long run the financial success of the Company did not depend on its operations in Guelph, Guelph did provide the example of a spectacular undertaking and a successful settlement.

2) Infrastructure

The company was aware of the importance of this factor in the Guelph settlement. The infrastructure which they introduced there consisted of roads which encouraged and preceded settlement, rather than following it; a local mill, which was a necessity if the settler was to have a market for his produce and still make a profit on his labours; and a school to attract settlers and provide an essential service. Galt was particularly influenced in this regard by the experience and operations of the Holland Land Company (1796-1837) in western New York state.

It is also interesting to examine the size of the Company's expenditures on infrastructure in the various parts of the province. For the Guelph settlement the ratio of a) the expenditures by the Company on improvements to b) the price paid by the Company to the government for the land was approximately 1:3/4. This high level of expenditure was largely the result of Galt's early emphasis on infrastructure. For the Huron Tract, this ratio was approximately 1:3, which was largely an expression of the Company's agreement with the British government to allow the Company to withhold one third of the purchase price for the Huron Tract lands, and to expend this amount of money in the Tract on improvements agreed to by the government of Upper Canada. For the Company's operations as a whole in Upper Canada, the ratio was approximately 1:6. This ratio was largely the result of the fact that more than half of the Company's land was scattered in 200 acre lots throughout Upper Canada, and, as a result, the Company made few, if any, improvements on these lands. Thus it can be seen that the Guelph settlement was fortunate in being initially provided with substantial infrastructure with which to integrate new settlers into the productive organization of the settlement, as well as prepare it for a larger regional role in the future.

3) Institutional Arrangements

Perhaps the most significant aspect of the institutional arrangements in relation to the Canada Company's operations was its use of agents and advertising and the provision of services to encourage emigration to Upper Canada. In March, 1827, the Court of Directors decided that it would be advisable to appoint agents at the various emigration ports of the British Isles as well as at Quebec and Montreal and to provide these agents with prospectuses of the Company and maps of the lands which were for sale in Upper Canada. As an encouragement to these agents, who were expected to forward emigrants with money to purchase lots, they were to receive one to two percent commissions. These commissions were paid on the basis of the money deposited with the Company, and money spent on the purchase of Company lands (cash or credit system) by these emigrants. The Company made arrangements with more than twenty agents in the British Isles in the period between 1827 and 1830 to act on the above basis. Main agencies (those usually listed on the Company's publicity material) in Scotland were located in Greenock, Glasgow, Edinburgh, Leith, Haddington and Aberdeen with a number of smaller agencies (those listed in newspaper shipping advertisements as representing the Company in the 1830s) in the Borders. Several of the agencies also received small cash payments as salaries. It became obvious that few emigrants while in the British Isles were prepared to enter into arrangements for the Company's land but rather preferred to wait until they had arrived in Upper Canada. After having inspected the areas for sale, they could choose land they wanted to buy. The Court of Directors recognized this as a reasonable wish on the part of the emigrants and decided in April 1831 that

> The appointment of Special Agents be in future discontinued and that a more broad and general principle of publicity be substituted by sending the Company's printed Papers at the beginning of every season to Ship Owners and Brokers connected with Canada Shipping both at London and the outports, and also to influential persons interested in emigration with an intimation that they may have more on application at the Office of the Company.[14]

Thus after 1831, there were only unofficial agencies operating at the larger emigration ports. The Company did for a short time employ an agent, William Cattermole, to visit various parts of Britain distributing Company literature and answering questions.[15] It should be noted, however, that even as late as 1841, Frederick Widder, one of the Company's Commissioners in Upper Canada, suggested in a report to the Directors that the

Company should re-establish the system of agents in the principal emigration ports in order to attract more settlers to purchase
the Company's lands. He advocated that in some cases it might
even be wise to pay emigrants' passages from Great Britain to
Quebec.[16] Nothing came of these ideas however.

As well as agents (both official and unofficial) attracting
emigrants to the Company's lands in Upper Canada, the Company carried on an extensive publicity campaign. Each of the
agents received maps and printed information about the
Company's lands; broadsides (large printed sheets) to be posted
in market towns and villages describing the advantages of emigration to Upper Canada; and copies of letters written by recent
emigrants to their friends or relatives at home in the British
Isles. The Company felt that "no description of evidence is
received with more confidence than that of emigrants themselves founded on a practical knowledge of the country. The
Board therefore will never spare the expense of printing, and
circulating intelligent letters".[17] An example of such a letter,
included with the Report of the Court of Directors for 1831, is
one from John Inglis, Guelph, Upper Canada, to John Younger,
a shoemaker in Roxburghshire, dated February 26, 1831. It
contained a detailed and favourable description of life and
conditions in Upper Canada, including

> Dear John, I would not just wish to advise any one to come
> here; but, for my own part, I would not return to Scotland,
> though any one would pay my passage back and give me
> twenty pounds a year,—not that I do not love the land of
> Caledonia, which will ever be dear to my bosom, (and I could
> knock down the man who speaks ill of it,) but I never could
> have the prospects for my family in Britain that I here have;
> only one thing is to be remarked, no one need come here in
> prospect of doing well unless he intend to be diligent, and
> work hard; and he who does so will, in the course of seven or
> eight years, feel independent.
> Dear John, how happy would I be to have you here, with
> my dear brother and sisters, and the sooner the better would it
> be for yourselves.[18]

Indeed over the period 1830 to 1842 the Company circulated at least 20,000 copies of various letters from settlers. The Company also purchased large numbers of books and pamphlets by various writers, on the advantages of emigration to Canada, for distribution in the British Isles.

The Canada Company also provided a number of services to emigrants as well as to established settlers. Although the Company did not become involved in the embarkation or passage of persons to Quebec, as they felt it could be carried on as easily and cheaply through the regular channels, they did offer a free passage from Quebec to the head of Lake Ontario beginning in 1827 to emigrants who paid the instalment on one hundred acres or more. In 1833, the last year in which this assistance was offered, it was restricted to settlers going to the Huron Tract.[19] The Company also acted, free of charge, as transfer agent for remittances of money from the British Isles to Canada or vice versa, using letters of credit.[20] The Company also operated a Settlers Savings Bank at which the Company's lessees received interest at six percent per annum on monies deposited, with the amount available without notice and interest accrued daily. The purpose was to encourage and assist the settler to accumulate money in order to purchase the land he was leasing.[21] As mentioned previously, the Company realized the importance of favourable reports sent home in emigrants' letters and decided to transmit these letters free of postage to friends at home, at least during the year 1831. With the emigrant's letter the Company enclosed a letter of its own, stating

I forward the enclosed Letter to you from your Friends in Canada who are Settlers on the Company's Lands, and shall be happy to send any Letters you may have for them also free of charge. I hope the accounts are good and shall be glad to have Extracts of any parts that are interesting to Persons intending to emigrate from this Country.[22]

The Company also provided formal letters of introduction to its Agents and Commissioners in Upper Canada for people who had the means and intention of buying lands from the Company, as well as for those people who were being sponsored by influential people in the British Isles.[23] All of these services would be of considerable assistance to emigrants, especially those of some means, and made the prospects of emigration seem much less formidable. As a result of its publicity campaign and general activities in Upper Canada, the Company received favourable comment in emigrant guides and Scottish newspapers.[24]

4) Transformation

Transformation involved the replacement of the single-commodity, export-based economy by diversification of production in which the urban units become independent forces rather than being completely dependent on agriculture. The role of the town of Guelph in the settlement scheme was of considerable importance. As the town of Guelph grew, it was affected by, and in turn had an influence upon, areas around it: Guelph Township, other surrounding townships, the area to the north, and the Huron Tract. From the beginning, Guelph town and township, were influenced by the same factors. The town served initially as an administrative base for the Canada Company, as a staging point prior to settlement of the land, as a commercial centre providing essential goods and services, and as a centre for social life on the forest fringe. The location of the town at an excellent waterpower site on the Speed River led early to the establishment of grist and sawmills.

It is felt that in the development of the Guelph settlement several very broad stages can be seen in the time period under examination.[25] The first, or the stage of pre-development, consisted of the early years up to about 1832. In this stage the settlement was founded and took shape under the direction of John Galt, with the Canada Company providing the impetus in the form of capital, organization, and infrastructure.

The second stage in the development of the Guelph settlement began in 1832 following the slump as a result of the Company cutting back on its expenditures and interest. However, during this stage, the Company continued to encourage immigration to the settlement, and soon all the farm land had been taken up. This is when development really began, progressing on the strength of the facilities provided in the first stage. The land was cleared, crops planted, and markets found. The production facilities of the town expanded using the excellent water power sites available. This was the stage of sweat and toil, of slow but steady growth.

Finally, the third and last stage, of maturity and self-sustaining growth, began in the early 1850s. The town had then become a regional centre both politically and economically. With the coming of the railways to Guelph in the late 1850s, the town's continued growth was assured and the manufacturing base which existed, diversified and expanded greatly.

Conclusion

Prior to 1825, the development of Upper Canada had been hesitant, and the government land alienation policies and various land settlement schemes had been far from successful. The initiation of the Canada Company was an attempt at achieving effective settlement and hence the growth and prosperity of the colony. The Company based its operations on capital, credit, infrastructure, and publicity, and in this manner developed the land resource that it had obtained. The Guelph settlement was the Company's first undertaking, with John Galt as the driving force. The town of Guelph was the centre piece. The town reacted with the Company and with its region and soon developed on the foundation laid by the Company into an important regional centre. The Company had provided organization and capital until the Guelph settlement could provide its own. Without a doubt, the increased immigration to Canada and the growing markets for wheat created a period of prosperity which benefitted the Company as well as the country, but it is felt that in general the methods and approaches used by the Company were nevertheless appropriate to the circumstances.

Notes

[1]Helen I. Cowan, *British Emigration to British North America* (University of Toronto Press, 1961), pp. 113-123.

[2]Gerald M. Craig, *Upper Canada/The Formative Years, 1784-1841* (Toronto, 1963), pp. 128-129. (For a discussion of the Peterborough settlement, see Brunger's paper, *supra*).

[3]Gerald M. Craig, *op. cit.*, pp. 130-1.

[4]Sir C.P. Lucas, *Lord Durham's Report on the Affairs of British North America*, Vol. III (Oxford: Clarendon Press, 1912), pp. 58-60.

[5]Canada Company, *Report of the Court of Directors to the Proprietors for 1830*, p. 4. *Annual Report of the Public Archives of Canada, 1935* (Ottawa, 1936), pp. 207-209, 213-15.

[6]Charles P. Kindleberger, *Economic Development* (Toronto: McGraw-Hill, 1965), p. 168.

[7]Joseph L. Fisher, "The Role of Natural Resources", *Economic Development—Principles and Patterns*, Harold F. Williamson and John A. Buttrick (Editors), (Englewood Cliffs, New Jersey: Prentice-Hall, 1955), p. 29.

[8]This process in the context of Southern Ontario is well documented in the following publications: Jacob Spelt, *Urban Development in South-Central Ontario*, Carleton Library No. 57 (Toronto, 1972). Peter G. Goheen, *Victorian Toronto, 1850-1900: Pattern and Process of Growth* (Chicago, 1970), especially Chapters 3 and 4.

[9]W.T. Easterbrook and H.G.J. Aitken, *Canadian Economic History* (Toronto: Macmillan, 1963), pp. 274-275.

[10]The three methods of acquiring land from the Canada Company were: (a) cash payment; (b) 1/5 cash and the remainder of the purchase money in five annual instalments, with interest; (c) a ten year lease, with no money down with the rents payable on each February 1st with option to purchase at a fixed price any time during the ten years; this policy was introduced in the Huron Tract in the mid-1840s. From *Guelph and Galt Advertiser and Wellington District Advocate*, August 29, 1845, No. 7, Vol. 1.

[11]"Sketches of the Settlement and Early History of Guelph and the Townships in the County of Wellington", compiled by the editor of the *Guelph Mercury* and published January-August 1866 (Ontario Archives).

[12]Canada Company, *Report of the Court of Directors to the Proprietors for 1831* (London: W. Marchant, 1832), p. 13. The Ontario Archives (Toronto) has the most complete collection available of Canada Company papers, including minute books, correspondence and land records.

[13]*Montreal Gazette*, May 7, 1832, Canada Company Advertisement from *Select Documents in Canadian Economic History, 1783-1885*, edited by H.A. Innis and A.R.M. Lower (Toronto, 1933), pp. 30-31.

[14]Canada Company, "Minutes of the Court of Directors", April 7, 1831.

[15]Robert C. Lee, "The Canada Company 1826-1853, A Study in Direction", unpublished M.A. thesis, University of Guelph, 1967, p. 105.

[16]Canada Company, "Letters to the Court of Directors from Frederick Widder", June 24, 1841.

[17]Canada Company, "Commissioners' Reports", February 12, 1831.

[18]Canada Company, *Report of the Court of Directors to the Proprietors for 1831*, London, March 1832.

[19]Clarence Karr, *The Canada Company and the Early Years*, Ontario Historical Society, Research Publication, No. 3, Ottawa, 1974, pp. 90-94.

[20]*Montreal Gazette*, May 7, 1832, in *Select Documents in Canadian Economic History, 1783-1885*, edited by H.A. Innis and A.R.M. Lower (Toronto, 1933), pp. 30-31. *Quebec Mercury*, May 8, 1832.

[21]*Guelph and Galt Advertiser and Wellington District Advocate*, August 29, 1845, No. 7., Vol. 1. In 1844 the Company remitted £4,141 12s 7d from 265 settlers.

[22]Canada Company, "Letter Book", March 11, 1831.

[23]Canada Company, "Correspondence with Commissioners", dated London June 28, 1832. Letter of introduction for the Rev. William Proudfoot, a Scottish clergyman "on a Mission of Enquiry into the State of the Religious Institutions of the Scotch" in Upper Canada.

[24]*Glasgow Herald*, August 24, 1827; July 15, 1842; February 17, 1843. *Aberdeen Journal*, September 28, 1853. *Paisley Advertiser*, September 2, 1826. *Chambers Information for the People*, (edited by William and Robert Chambers), No. 1 (London and Edinburgh, 1835).

[25]W.W. Rostow, *The Process of Economic Growth* (New York: Norton and Co., 1952), Chapter 4. Harvey S. Perloff, *et al.*, *Regions, Resources and Economic Growth* (Baltimore: Johns Hopkins Press, 1960), pp. 58-60.

9. KINGSTON IN THE NINETEENTH CENTURY: A STUDY IN URBAN DECLINE

Brian S. Osborne

Commenting on the future of Kingston in 1791, Patrick Campbell noted that "everything is inviting, and it seems by nature intended for emporium of this new country, capable of being extended to a considerable empire".[1] In 1842, these promises seem to have been realized and the editor of a local newspaper was able to underscore the reasons for the continued prosperity of Kingston:

> Here centres the export and import trades of the Great Lakes, the River St. Lawrence and Rideau Canal.—Here is fixed the Seat of the Provincial Government of United Canada, the most flourishing Colony of the British Empire. —Kingston is the strongest Naval and Military Post above Quebec—and the acknowledged key of Western Canada. When all these natural and acquired advantages are considered, we cease to wonder at the rapid rise and importance of this City.[2]

By 1864, however, a different picture was emerging and a contemporary visitor to the city observed:

> Kingston has seen better days, for it could hardly fall upon worse or more gloomy days . . . I do not know the exact period in the history of Kingston when melancholy marked it for its own; but if one may judge by the length of the grass in the streets, it can hardly be within the recollection of the existing generation.[3]

That the initial optimistic assessments were not realized; that the early dominance of Kingston was not maintained; and that Kingston experienced a significant relative decline in the nineteenth century urban hierarchy of Ontario, constitutes one of the most interesting aspects of the urban history of the province.

The Evolving Hierarchy

Any analysis of the settlement of a frontier region cannot be complete without a consideration of the urban nodes that were associated with its development. For much of the early nineteenth century, Upper Canada was still a frontier society characterized by a sparse population, a subsistence agricultural economy and, therefore, but limited trade and commerce. However, the basic pattern of distribution of nascent urban centres had been already established. The earliest of these centres were initiated as military, administrative or commercial outposts during the preliminary stage of the pioneer settlement. Others developed later as the settlement of the region progressed and generated the need for local service centres. To this extent, a certain inertia is apparent in that the spatial pattern produced at the very outset of the settlement process was to be found but little altered at the close of the century. However, a vertical dynamism was imparted to this picture as the differential growth rates of the urban centres produced significant changes in the evolving hierarchy. The growth potential of each was influenced by the character and properties of the initial location, the ability to attract diverse functions, the degree of productivity of the hinterland, and the capacity for adjusting to extraneous factors.

In 1783, the need for a centre for settling the displaced Loyalists and a naval base to replace Carleton Island recently acquired by the U.S. focussed British attention upon the former French settlement of Fort Frontenac. In that year, Major Ross and some 370 soldiers prepared the site of the future city of Kingston. With the arrival of the settlers in 1784, the population rose to 2,000 but soon dropped to 400 as the majority were located on lands throughout the surrounding area. At the commencement of the nineteenth century, Kingston was the leading settlement with important military, commercial and trade functions while York, the capital of the province, was second in importance. The 1812 war consolidated Kingston's lead over the other emerging urban centres in Upper Canada. Gourlay noted that "Though the war destroyed Niagara, checked the progress of York and made Earnesttown 'a deserted village' it doubled the population, the buildings, and business of Kingston."[4] Kingston was still the premier settlement of the province in 1830, at which time there were five towns with populations in excess of 1,000: Kingston (3,587), York (2,800), London (2,415), Hamilton (2,013), Brockville (1,130).[5] For most of the first half of the nineteenth century, Kingston was able to maintain this lead, its function as a military centre and port was consolidated, while even political power became centred in the city in 1841. Continued growth was thought to be assured and would "in half a century, cause it to become one of the greatest cities of the freshwater seas."[6]

The second half of the nineteenth century, however, was to see the more rapid development of the westerly sections of the province and the rise to dominance of their urban centres. The initial basis for this had been prepared by the increased migration to the western districts and the progress of the agricultural economy of that area. Thus, as early as the 1829-1835 period, when Kingston's Midland District experienced a population increase of only 11 percent, the Home District centred on York increased by some 128 percent.[7] The import of these figures was fully appreciated by some Kingston interests and they were concerned that their town would become "a 'deserted village', notwithstanding the many advantages it possesses; while the forests of the West produce new ones [towns] daily like mushrooms."[8] By the mid-century, Toronto (30,775) had risen to the position of urban dominance in Canada West, but Kingston (11,697) had fallen to third position behind Hamilton (14,112). Kingston fared no better in the ensuing decade experiencing the lowest rate of population increase (17.5 percent) of the five top centres, and declining to fourth rank in the hierarchy. By this time, Kingston had recognized the loss of its capital function, had had a foretaste of the effect of the departure of the military, and was beginning to be aware of the factors that were to eventually weaken its port function. Between 1861 and

1871, Kingston dropped one more place in the hierarchy, experiencing an absolute population loss of some 9.7 percent at a time when the four higher ranking centres all experienced growth in excess of 25 percent. While Kingston was able to maintain this ranking until the close of the century, it fell farther behind the leading centres in terms of population. Thus, by 1901, Toronto with its 208,040 people had emerged as the metropolitan dominant of the provincial hierarchy, while Kingston at 17,961 was relegated to the position of a satellite city, significant only to an ever constricting hinterland.[9]

D.C. Masters, commenting on this spectacular rise to dominance by Toronto, observes that "the 1850-1890 period is decisive in Toronto's triumph over other Ontario rivals."[10] The corollary of this absolute growth of Toronto was the relative demise of Kingston during the same period. Kingston's failure to maintain its initial advantages and to embark upon a period of self-sustaining growth is best explained in the context of the changing fortunes of the city's three major functions in the nineteenth century. The loss of the military, the failure to attract the capital, and the decline of the port all occurred in the second half of the nineteenth century. These factors, in conjunction with the poorly developed local hinterland, are closely related to the relative decline of Kingston.

Kingston as Military Centre

At successive periods in its history, Kingston has been on the political frontier between the French and the Iroquois, the French and the British, and the British and the Americans. During each of these periods of potential and actual political conflict, Kingston has been developed as a major centre of fortification and has played a significant role in, and been influenced by, the military activities centred on this city.[11]

The French first recognized the strategic value of the site and, in 1673, Count Frontenac established a fort for the control of the Iroquois and the propagation of the fur trade. Refurbished in 1695, it attained a new significance in the eighteenth century as an outpost facing the British on the Mohawk River. Following the assertion of British control over the area in 1763, Fort Frontenac was neglected until 1783 when the naval base was transferred from Carleton Island and fortifications constructed. At the commencement of the 1812 war, the military significance of Kingston as a fortified centre and naval base was such that it was considered by the U.S. to be:

. . . the great depot of his [the enemy's] resources. So long as he retains this and keeps open his communications with the sea, he will not want the means for multiplying his naval and other defences and of reinforcing or renewing war in the west.[12]

Kingston was protected by the construction of a wooden palisade and blockhouses, fortifications on Point Henry, and a garrison of 2,000 men.

Following the 1812 war, Britain established a line of fortified posts extending some 860 miles between Detroit in the west and Riviere du Loup in the east to contain the feared expansion of the U.S. Kingston's strategic location as a naval dockyard, garrison town and transport centre was such that by 1822 it was considered that "next to Quebec and Halifax it is the strongest post in all British America."[13] The initial military development had consisted of an upgrading of the existing fortifications, and the construction of the Rideau Canal to link Lake Ontario and Montreal via the Ottawa River to avoid the vulnerable St. Lawrence. However, in 1825, the Bryce Committee, appointed by the Board of Ordnance, recommended an elaborate scheme of some six redoubts, together with supporting Martello towers. Eventually, one of the redoubts, Fort Henry, was constructed. Additional construction was undertaken during the Oregon crisis of 1841-48 when four Martello towers and associated batteries were constructed. (See Figure 9.1).[14] Throughout most of this period, the garrison fluctuated around 1,500 men and these, together with their dependents constituted a significant proportion of the population of the developing town. With the closing of the naval dockyard in 1853 and the withdrawal of the troops for the Crimean War, the town experienced the foretaste of the final withdrawal of the military in 1870. This was to constitute a severe blow to the city as the military had made a significant contribution to the economy of Kingston.

While the construction of fortifications had been effected at

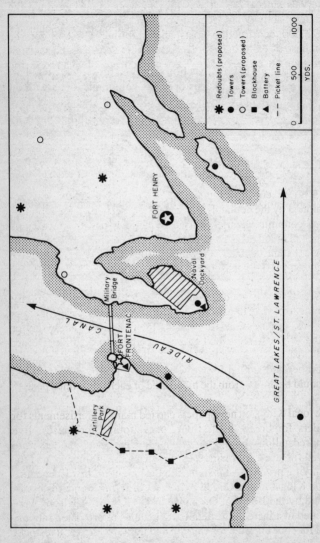

9.1 Kingston fortifications, 1673-1871.

intervals since 1783, it was the 1828 plan that generated the greatest activity in Kingston. The original estimate was £273,000 construction costs and a further £97,848 for the purchase of 1,958 acres of land at £50 per acre.[15] Land speculation soon raised the price to £500 per acre and the plan for a ring of fortifications around Kingston was abandoned. However, Fort Henry was constructed at a cost of £70,000 while the call for tenders for additional defences in 1846 injected a further five million dollars into the local economy for additions to, and repair of the fortifications.[16] The construction was effected by local companies and it was anticipated that "these works will cause a circulation during the next year of some £60-70,000 so that somebody will benefit from the expenditures."[17]

A more constant input into the city's economy was occasioned by the demands generated by the garrison for supplies. The economic vagaries caused by depressions and recessions which plagued other parts were lessened in Kingston because of this constant demand. Phip has itemized the type of supplies required by the garrisons:

> The physical goods needed to keep these isolated military units in a state of efficiency were of two kinds. Such items as arms, ammunition, rum for the men's rations, and wine for the officer's table had to be imported from Europe, other British colonies, or the U.S. On the other hand, beef, flour, timber and animal forage were typical frontier products and could be drawn from the hinterland of each garrisoned post.[18]

The local Kingston newspapers carried many advertisements for tenders for bread, beef, flour, peas, forage for horses, five hundred gallons of drinking water a day, etc. Other tenders were called for straw for mattresses, for sweeping chimneys, and for emptying privies. An insight into the extent of this dependence upon Kingston is afforded by the set of living standards established by the Board of Ordnance in 1841.[19] All garrisons were obliged to adhere to the detailed schedules of provision rations, fuel for cooking, fuel for warmth and light, fodder for livestock, etc. Since the complement of the garrison is also known for this period, and since prices may be obtained from the contemporary newspapers, an assessment of the degree of the garrison's commercial dependence upon the community may be attempted.

Thus, the annual demands for heat, light, bread and meat were as follows:

Fuel	4,640 cords	@ 8/-	£ 1,856
Light	8,000 lbs.	6d	200
Flour	1,680 barrels	22/6	1,862
Beef/Pork	3,650 cwts.	—	2,803

The demand for flour alone constituted a significant market for local farms. The 1,680 barrels of flour represented some 5,488 bushels of wheat per annum. Assuming an average yield of 15 bushes per acre, the demand for flour, therefore, supported some 365 acres of land under wheat. The extent to which this demand benefited local farmers or merchants is a different proposition, however, as local agents of Montreal merchants were able to underbid local competitors. It was this that motivated a contemporary observer·to comment that the garrison was "independent and apart from the agricultural community."[20]

Another important military contribution to Kingston's economy consisted of the wages paid to the garrison. In 1841 these were:

N.C.O.s and men	£ 15,470-0-0
Staff sgts.	182-0-0
Officers	5,491-0-0
Field officers	428-5-0[21]

Much of this total of £21,571-5-0 was expended on goods and services in Kingston but the form of this commercial dependence was considered by many to be a mixed blessing:

> The presence of so many soldiers has a demoralizing influence especially in the multiplication of bar taverns and groggeries which spring up like mushrooms in the vicinity of the garrison, scattering liberally the germs of misery and degradation.[22]

With the departure of the military in 1870, Kingston received a significant setback. Not only did it occasion an absolute loss in population, but it also had a pronounced effect on the economy of the town. The military expenditures had been borne by Great Britain at no cost to the province and Kingston had been the recipient of the direct benefits. The construction of the fortifications provided both employment and stimulated local businesses. The garrison constituted a considerable market for local produce and a user of the various services provided by the city. The artificiality of the economic contribution made by the military had been mooted earlier by local observers and the point had been made that ''£1000 would be better spent on the macadamization of a road than many thousands occasioned by the troops and officers in the garrison.''[23] Moreover, while the presence of the military undoubtedly infused substantial amounts of money into the local economy, it is to be questioned whether this served to diminish local business initiative.

Kingston as Capital

Despite Kingston's initial momentum following 1783 and its continued lead as a mercantile and military centre, it was not chosen as the capital of the new province in 1791. Newark, and later York, were the preferred cities and it was not until fifty years later that Kingston again claimed the function of capital city.

Following the Act of Union of 1840, Kingston was one of the cities considered for the capital of the united provinces. Even before the final decision was made, there was considerable excitement in the city:

> There are no unoccupied tenements in town, rents are quite high and houses are in great demand. This is partially due to the rumours mentioned above (that Upper and Lower Canada will unite soon with Kingston as the Capital).[24]

On February 6, 1841, Lord Sydenham finally announced his selection of Kingston as the capital, much to the chagrin of both Montreal and Toronto.[25] Kingston's harbour was thought to be too small, too unprotected and frozen too long, while the city was deficient in both housing and supplies. On the other hand, there were several reasons for selecting Kingston. Loyalty during the rebellions of the 1830s, the significant array of military defences, transport connections with both Canada East and Canada West, the accessibility of all parts of the town to the central government offices, and the personal committment of Lord Sydenham to Kingston, were all pressing arguments.

Parliament met in Kingston on May 26, 1841, and the associated addition of some 3,000 officials, dependents and servants to the base population of 6,000 placed much strain on the existing accommodation, supplies and services.[26] The demand for housing produced a building boom characterised by construction on lots smaller than the earlier accepted models because of the inflated land prices. However, the pressure on the facilities of the city were such that the capital was transferred to Montreal in November, 1843. Inadequate housing, food shortages, and the fear of conflict with the U.S. over the "54°40' or fight" election campaign of 1843 all militated against Kingston.

The loss of the capital function resulted in an immediate drop in population and an associated social and economic depression:

> Kingston appears as may be expected, dull and flat. That a very serious injury has been inflicted upon some individuals who have been induced to spend money on building houses—even probably to their ruin—is most certain; that others will suffer from reduced incomes and that all, more or less, feel the consequences cannot be denied.[27]

Despite these repercussions, Kingston continued to put forward claims for the seat of government until the decision to establish it at Ottawa was recognized in 1858.[28] While this loss of the capital function was not a sufficient cause for the decline of the city, it could be regarded as symptomatic of the failing fortunes of Kingston at this time.

Kingston as a Port

Writing in 1855, C.R. Weld observed that "Removal of the seat of government from Kingston has had a most injurious effect on the town and yet it is admirably suited for commerce."[29] If, in the nineteenth century, Kingston had claims to being a centre of military significance and pretentions of political dominance, it should be emphasized that its primary function continued to be that of port and transhipment point for the Lake Ontario-St. Lawrence traffic. The fundamental pattern of the economic organization of the St. Lawrence-Great Lakes region in the nineteenth century was the movement of goods to the warehouses and wharves of the dominant economic interests both at Montreal and Quebec. The logic of Kingston's properties of site and situation rendered it an important satellite port of these interests and stimulated various activities associated with the break-in-bulk function.

Situated at the junction of the St. Lawrence and Lake Ontario, Kingston was long the place of transhipment between two different systems of water transport. For both the French in the eighteenth century and the British in the early nineteenth century, this had meant the shifting of cargoes from Lake Ontario schooners to St. Lawrence canoes, batteaux and rafts. The construction of the Rideau Canal furthered this function since it consisted of a series of canals, drowned lands and inland lakes which were not serviced by tow paths and were not suited to sail. The use of the canal, therefore, required transhipment from the schooners and steam boats of the lake to the steam-hauled barges of the canal. The initial effect of the St. Lawrence improvements also emphasized Kingston's function by requiring the transfer of cargoes to the specialized canalers of the St. Lawrence system. Similarly, the first reaction of Kingston to rail transport was to attempt to develop it as a tributary system to the main water transport system and so augment the total traffic passing through Kingston.

The characteristics of Kingston's site also met the specialized requirements of the process of transhipment of the commodities being transferred at the port. During the late eighteenth and early nineteenth centuries, a miscellany of primary products left the area, including furs, lumber, naval stores, potash, wheat, flour and salted meats. These diversified cargoes were accommodated by the adequate waterfront facilities of the then commodious harbour. Early in the nineteenth century, however, while the commodities continued to be diverse, lumber and grain increasingly dominated Kingston's traffic. The assemblage of "drams" into rafts required a quiet water area, as did the transfer of grain from schooners and lakers to canalers and barges. Kingston harbour and its adjacent waters were suitable in that they were close to the St. Lawrence system, and yet undisturbed by its currents.

With these peculiar advantages, Kingston early established itself as an important port of the St. Lawrence-Lake Ontario navigation system. As early as 1800, Kingston's twelve merchants shipped out 238 boat loads of flour, wheat, potash and various other primary products of the frontier. In 1815, J. Bouchette observed:

> For the last fifteen years the town has obtained considerable mercantile importance; wharfs have been constructed, and many spacious warehouses erected, that are usually filled with merchandise: in fact it is now become the main entrepot between Montreal and all the settlements along the lakes to the westward.[30]

This prosperity continued to the mid-nineteenth century as both the export and import trade flourished. The waterfront was extended, new wharves constructed and several forwarding companies were based at the port. The latter constituted the key to the transhipment industry and in 1863 there were seven such agencies based at Kingston, each with its own fleet of lakers, barges and tugs, and facilities for docking, handling and storage. During the same period, some thirty steam and fifty sailing ships wintered in Kingston, constituting the largest fleet of vessels on Lake Ontario at this date.[31]

A variety of related activities were associated with Kingston's port function. The 1861 census refers to such activities as boatmen, boatbuilders, ferrymen, mariners, sailors, pilots, shipwrights, chandlers, builders, wharfingers, fishermen, sailmakers etc. Still others classified as labourers were employed in the various yards and foundries. Shipbuilding played a particularly important role in the economic structure of Kingston and by 1871, of the twenty-nine shipyards in the province, eight were located in the Kingston area, constructing and repairing the barges, lakers and canalers using the port.[32] Over ninety percent of the ships registered at Kingston between 1840 and 1890, were built in the fifty shipbuilding centres that operated in the Kingston area during this period.[33] The larger shipyards of Kingston, Portsmouth, and Garden Island domi-

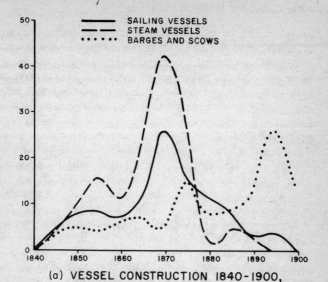

(a) VESSEL CONSTRUCTION 1840-1900,
KINGSTON AND RIDEAU CANAL AREA

SAILING VESSELS
STEAM VESSELS
BARGES AND SCOWS

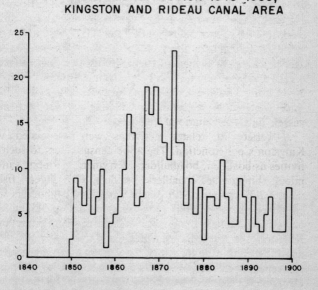

9.2 a) Vessel construction, 1840-1900, Kingston and Rideau Canal
area; b) Ship registration, Kingston, 1840-1900. Both from
Canada Shipping Register.

nated this activity, but tributary centres were established along the waters of the Rideau Canal and Bay of Quinte as local timber resources were depleted. As ships and barges grew larger, and as sail was replaced by steam, the trend in the industry was away from individual "yeomen" shipwrights, who were often itinerant, to the larger shipbuilding companies concentrated on Kingston. The latter were typically larger units with dry docks and specialized repair facilities. Kingston's initial advantage had been the local timber resources, a skilled labour force derived from the former naval dockyards, and association with local shipping interests. As ships increased in size, and with the shift from wooden to iron vessels, so the local shipbuilding industry also declined. (See Figure 9.2a).

The decline of Kingston as a shipbuilding centre was also associated with the general decline of the port function. One indication of this decline was the decrease in the number of ships registered at Kingston during the 1870s. (See Figure 9.2b). Thus, the annual report of the Department of Inland Revenue for 1871 noted that the "transhipment of grain at Kingston during the present season assumed very larger proportions" but also commented that:

> Of the grain thus far brought to Lake Ontario the greater part has gone to Kingston. . . . I may mention that the quantity of grain requiring transhipment at Kingston during the present season has been at times largely in excess of the means which exist for doing the business.[34]

However, the general trade figures for the port for the latter part of the nineteenth century show trade to be continuing to increase, if at a much slower rate than that of the other Lake Ontario ports. (See Table 9.1).[35]

Several reasons account for Kingston's failure to maintain its specialized function as transhipment port for the Great Lakes-St. Lawrence traffic.

Firstly, the initial serious blow dealt to Kingston's trade in flour and grain was occasioned by the repeal of the British Corn Laws in 1846 and the revocation of the Navigation Acts in 1849. Under the system of Free Trade, there was no advantage to be gained from shipping via Canadian ports and the U.S. wheat

TABLE 9.1

Port Trade, Kingston and Toronto, 1851-1901

KINGSTON

Year	Exports Value	Imports Value	Duty Value	% Incr.
1851	$ 132,188	$ 606,128	$ 69,000	
1861	415,081	4,487,587	97,792	41.72
1871	1,435,404	7,923,378	136,388	39.46
1881	1,050,875	1,183,424	184,066	34.95
1891	715,628	1,231,628	126,278	−31.39
1901	133,696	1,245,841	146,508	16.02

TORONTO

Year	Exports Value	Imports Value	Duty Value	% Incr.
1851	$ 327,404	$ 2,713,972	$ 377,320	
1861	1,467,947	4,619,149	588,652	56.01
1871	2,118,978	10,354,265	1,546,101	162.65
1881	3,455,108	15,090,629	3,136,446	102.86
1891	3,500,642	19,343,968	4,076,928	29.98
1901	314,268	31,803,016	5,306,416	30.15

henceforth moved via Buffalo and the Erie Canal rather than
Kingston and the St. Lawrence. New York was nearer, open
longer and characterized by cheaper freight rates to Europe than
Montreal. Kingston for long handled much of the traffic that did
flow to Montreal, but this too was to be diminished by other
factors.

Secondly, by 1847, the St. Lawrence rapids had been by-
passed by a series of canals which allowed navigation by boats
of nine feet draught. The implication of this development on
Kingston's transhipment function was recognized immediately:

What effect the opening of the St. Lawrence Canals and the
enlarging of the locks of the Welland Canal, will have upon it
remains to be seen. Hitherto, all the up and down freight has
been transhipped to Kingston, to either larger or smaller
vessels according as it has been going up or down; in carrying

which a fleet of about two hundred barges and schooners, of
from sixty to two hundred and fifty tons burthen, has been
employed. As soon as the improvements in canals are completed, large vessels will be enabled to run direct from
Montreal to Toronto and Hamilton, thus avoiding Kingston
altogether.[36]

Initially, however, the canals with their specialized navigational
requirements had at first augmented Kingston's break-in-bulk
function. Thus, the Royal Mail Line advertised in 1853 that

The Steamers of this line have been built expressly, and with
greatest care, for Lake and River Navigation; the River
Steamers with a Draft of Water, rendering the greatest security in descending the rapids; while the Lake Steamers are
large, staunch, and commodious, with powerful engines;
securing to travellers the greatest safety and comfort in all
weathers. They are filed [sic] up with Saloons and State
rooms elegantly furnished, and in point of speed
unsurpassed.[37]

However, as the canals improved, so the larger vessels were
able to negotiate the St. Lawrence also and eventually travel
directly to the oceans. Kingston was increasingly relegated to
the function of a local port serving the schooners and smaller
lakers that continued to operate on Lake Ontario into the twentieth century.

Thirdly, railroads challenged the dominance of water transport and, therefore, weakened the position of towns with a
heavy dependence upon shipping. As already noted, Kingston
at first expected that rail connections would be complementary
to the shipping function and expected an increase in transhipment activities with the addition of goods transhipped from rail
to water transport. The chief concern was that with the construction of the railroad into Upper New York state in the 1840s,
ports such as Cape Vincent, Clayton, Ogdensburg and Sacketts
Harbour, with their rail link to Boston and New York added to
their existing shipping connections, would capture Kingston's
transhipment function. Accordingly, Kingston businessmen
supported the Kingston and Toronto Railroad Company which

was incorporated in 1846 to construct a bridge across Wolfe Island to Cape Vincent to link with the Rome-Waterton-Oswego railroad.[38] The corporation failed in 1851, but the concept was revitalized in the form of canal link across Wolfe Island to Cape Vincent when rail reached the latter in 1852. The new concept was to make Kingston the transhipment point for Lake Ontario traffic to New York rail system:

> The terminus of the railway was to be at Kingston where freight sheds would be constructed to receive goods. The freight cars would be loaded in Kingston and transported to Cape Vincent, via the canal, by railway car ferry.[39]

This route to Boston would be 121 miles shorter than the Ogdensburg-Boston link and was, therefore, expected to attract traffic from Georgian Bay, lumber from the Kingston hinterland to Albany and Troy, and much general traffic. Thus, with the approach of the Grand Trunk Railway in 1856, Kingston had cause to expect that it would link both the New York Central Railroad and the Grand Trunk system and so become an important terminus of the U.S. and Canadian network.

The reality of the advent of rail was a severe challenge to many smaller ports and especially Kingston which was initially by-passed by the G.T.R. Apart from freight traffic, Kingston was also involved in providing daily links with Cobourg, Port Hope, Darlington, Toronto, Hamilton, Queenstown and Montreal and less frequent connections with Ottawa, Oswego, Ogdensburg and Cape Vincent. The first element to be challenged was this carriage of passengers, mail and perishables and the effect was immediate. But while the G.T.R. soon attracted this traffic, the freight rate per ton continued to favour water transport of bulk cargoes which, for the first few years of competition, continued to be stored in Kingston warehouses for spring shipment. However, while lake shipping continued to flourish by handling these bulk cargoes, the trend towards larger and more specialized carriers eventually resulted in the by-passing and neglect of Kingston.

Finally, the development of shipbuilding technology furthered, the improvements of the St. Lawrence allowed, and competition with railroads required, an increase in the size of vessels on the St. Lawrence-Great Lakes system. Thus, by the end of the nineteenth century, many of the lakers had increased to 3,000 tons burden. An important implication of this trend was that Kingston's harbour was no longer capable of accommodating many of the ships plying the Great Lakes. The harbour had always been limited by its exposure to the south-westerly gales, its relatively late opening date, and the presence of two shoals of six and ten feet depth. As early as 1861, the construction of a break-water was suggested to increase the anchorage to 250 acres at a cost of £15,000 while attempts were made later to remove the obstructing shoals in the harbour.[40] However, the port facilities and harbour, while suited to the lake traffic of an earlier era, were increasingly unsuited to the larger units of the late nineteenth century and early twentieth century.

The Search for Alternatives

In the latter half of the nineteenth century, therefore, Kingston suffered from the new political and economic attitudes of the U.K. to Canada, the development of new transport systems and their associated flow patterns, and the new orientation of economic and political influence throughout the province. After the mid-nineteenth century, it became increasingly apparent that Kingston, if it were to experience continued growth, needed to replace its three former functions: the military, the capital, the port. The illusion of national, and even provincial, dominance was now laid to rest and in its place Kingston sought to establish some degree of regional influence.

In the past, Kingston had been so dependent upon its substantial, if ephemeral, initial advantages of the garrison, capital and port that it had neglected the development of its immediate hinterland to the north. As early as 1822, Gourlay had observed that "Kingston is subject to one local disadvantage, the want of a populous back country."[41] A decade later, a local observer commented shrewdly, "A Rideau may form a Bytown, and an Erie Canal a Rochester, but without an agricultural country they will soon arrive at their best days and then retrograde by degrees to insignificance."[42] Kingston's failure to settle the "back country'' was attributed partly to the quality of the land in the rear townships but it was argued by the promoters of the town that:

> It has been long acknowledged to be a great drawback, that we have no fertile back country to support us. The extensive trade carried on at Toronto is maintained by the rich country in the rear of it. . . . There is bad land, indeed, but three fourths of the whole is positively good, and much of this excellent. It only requires to be better known, in order to be extensively settled.[43]

If there was some good land, however, it did not attract the immigrants passing through Kingston to stay in this area. The need for a local Emigrant Society to promote the settlement of the town's hinterland was apparent:

> While in other portions of the Province, the inhabitants are indefatigable in their invitations to settlers; in our vicinity, everything seems ''to sleep on''; and Emigrants, instead of coming among us, are most certain to go by us, often for the reason that they were not even asked to stay.[44]

The major deficiency, however, was the absence of an effective system of communications on Kingston's landward side. Without this, those settlers who may have wished to stay in the area could not travel to that land which was thought to be suited to settlement. Accordingly, in 1835, the Grand Jury for the Midland District recommended the construction of four roads some fifty miles into the interior. These were to be chopped and cleared for a width of twenty five feet, with ten feet in the centre chopped clear to the ground.[45] While this plan was not realized immediately, by the middle of the century, some six turnpike roads had been constructed from Kingston to various adjacent townships.[46] With the advent of the system of northern colonization roads in the 1850s, Kingston's hinterland was extended approximately one hundred miles into the newly opened Ottawa-Huron tract of lumber and frontier agriculture. The potential of railroads in developing this northern hinterland was

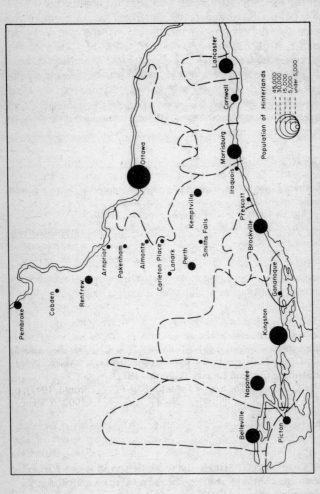

9.3 The hinterlands of market centres in eastern Ontario, 1881. From Ontario Agricultural Commission report, 1881.

also recognized, but of the dozen or so railroads proposed, only one, the Kingston-Pembroke, was actually constructed.

Kingston's expansion of its hinterland into a northern resource area did not provide the counter-effect to the declining fortunes of the city and was destined to failure. The northern experiment was effected in an area of limited agricultural potential, ephemeral resources and but transitory settlement. By the close of the nineteenth century, Kingston's future as the local metropolis of a declining region was clearly established. (See Figure 9.3).

Notes

[1] Patrick Campbell, *Travels in the Interior Inhabited Parts of North America in the Year 1791 and 1792* (Edinburgh, 1793), p. 142.

[2] *Kingston Chronicle and Gazette*, June 1, 1842.

[3] F. Duncan, *Our Garrisons in the West or Sketches in British North America* (London, 1864), p. 192.

[4] R. Gourlay, *A Statistical Account of Upper Canada* (London, 1822), Vol. 1, p. 128.

[5] Public Archives of Canada, R.G. 5, B. 26, Vol. 2.

[6] R.S. Bonnycastle, *The Canadas in 1841* (London, 1841), 2 vols., p. 120.

[7] Public Archives of Canada, R.G. 5, B. 26, Vol. 2.

[8] *Kingston Chronicle and Gazette*, July 11, 1835.

[9] *Census of Canada*, 1851-2, 1861-2, 1871-2, 1901. See also J. Spelt, *Urban Development in South-Central Ontario* (Assen, 1955), reprinted the Carleton Library (Toronto, 1972).

[10] D.C. Masters, *The Rise of Toronto 1850-1890* (Toronto, 1947), p. 2. See also Goheen, P., *Victorian Toronto, 1850-1900* (Chicago, 1970).

[11] W.A. Lavell, "A History of the Present Fortifications at Kingston," *Papers and Records, Ontario Historical Society*, Vol. XXXI, pp. 155-178.

[12] Quoted in F.G. Stanley and R.A. Preston, *A Short History of Kingston as a Military and Naval Centre* (Kingston, 1950), p. 9.

[13] Gourlay, *op. cit.*, p. 99.

[14] R.L. Way and B.W. Way, *Kingston's Defences 1783-1871*, Fort Henry Source Material, Old Fort Henry, Kingston.

[15] Way, *Kingston's Defences. . . .*

[16] Way, *Kingston's Defences. . . .*

[17]*Kingston Chronicle and Gazette*, January 30, 1846.

[18]J. Phip, "The Economic and Social Effects of the British Garrisons in the Development of Western Upper Canada", *Papers and Records, Ontario Historical Society*, Vol. 41, No. 1 (1949), p. 38.

[19]Board of Ordnance, *Condensed Schedule of Authorized Pay and Allowances in Canada, 1841* (Quebec, 1841).

[20]C.W. Cooper, *Frontenac, Lennox and Addington: An Essay* (Kingston, 1856), p. 21.

[21]Board of Ordnance, *op. cit.*

[22]A.M. Machar, *The Story of Kingston* (Toronto 1908), p. 153.

[23]Cooper, *Frontenac, Lennox. . .* , p. 17.

[24]*Kingston Chronicle and Gazette*, March 11, 1840.

[25]See J.E. Hodges, "The Civil Service when Kingston was the capital of Canada", *Historic Kingston*, Vol. 5, 1956.

[26]*Picton Gazette*, February 15, 1841.

[27]*Kingston Chronicle and Gazette*, June 14, 1843.

[28]*Kingston Chronicle and News*, April 23, 1858. Editorial comments that Ottawa definitely to be capital.

[29]C.R. Weld, *A Vacation Tour in the United States and Canada* (London, 1855), p. 91.

[30]J. Bouchette, *A Topographical Description of the Province of Lower Canada, with Remarks upon Upper Canada* (London, 1815), p. 599.

[31]*Kingston Chronicle and News*, February 3, 1860.

[32]*Census of Canada*, 1871.

[33]Canada Shipping Registers, Kingston 1846-1908.

[34]*Sessional Papers*, Fifth Session of First Parliament of Canada, 1872, Vol. No. 5, Paper No. 6, "Report of the Minister of Inland Revenue for 1871," p. 10.

[35]Tables of Trade and Navigation of Provinces of Canada.

       Sessional Papers, 1854-55, Vol. XIII
       Sessional Papers, 1863, Vol. I, No. 2
       Sessional Papers, 1872, Vol. V, No. 3
       Sessional Papers, 1882, Vol. XV, No. 1
       Sessional Papers, 1892, Vol. XXV, No. 4
       Sessional Papers, 1902, Vol. XXXVI, No. 11.

[36]W.H. Smith, *Canadian Gazetteer* (Toronto, 1846), p. 91.

[37]*Kingston British Whig*, July 29, 1853.

[38]Wolfe Island, Kingston and Toronto Railroad Company incorporated by 1846, 10 Victoria, Cap. CVIII.

[39]*Kingston Daily News*, June 19, 1852.

[40]*Kingston Chronicle and News*, April 12, 1861.

[41]Gourlay, *op. cit.*, p. 128.

[42]*Kingston Chronicle and Gazette*, August 26, 1835.

[43]*Ibid.*, November 15, 1834.

[44]*Ibid.*, September 21, 1833.

[45]*Ibid.*, August 8, 1835.

[46]T. Flynn, *Directory of the City of Kingston, 1857-1858* (Toronto, 1858), pp. 271-272.

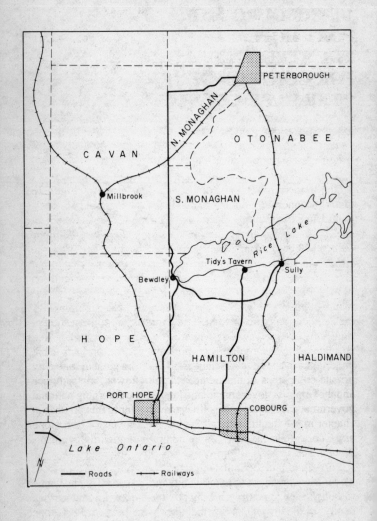

10.1 Principal transport lines between Port Hope, Cobourg, and Peterborough, to 1860.

10. COBOURG AND PORT HOPE: THE STRUGGLE FOR CONTROL OF "THE BACK COUNTRY"

Peter Ennals

The modern observer of the human landscape of Southern Ontario cannot fail to notice remnants of the Upper Canadian's confidence in the future greatness of the new land and the new society. In every corner of "Old Ontario" there are buildings both public and private which were built to a scale and in a style which we now associate with the heady spirit of Victorian expansiveness and optimism, the period that mid-Victorian writers lauded as the "age of improvement".[1] One of the manifestations of this spirit was a mania for "internal improvements", a synonym for the development of more efficient transport facilities, which began with roads and canals and culminated in the building of railways. These projects were undertaken at a variety of scales, ranging from those initiated by private companies to those undertaken by towns, the province and the Imperial government, and later by the emerging national government. This paper describes one chapter in this process, a chapter involving the struggle between the towns of Port Hope and Cobourg for the control of a common hinterland by means of such transportation improvements. (See Figure 10.1).

Port Hope and Cobourg are but seven miles apart yet both places developed concurrently and for essentially the same reasons. Each appeared early as the local entrepot and service centre for the townships in which they were located. Port Hope is known to have been the site of a Mississauga Indian village and trading point and was the southern terminus of the Ganaraska Portage.[2] There is no evidence that Cobourg was occupied before the region was first thrown open to settlers in

183

1792. At that time the two townships of Hope and Hamilton were among those made available by Lieutenant-Governor Simcoe to groups of associates who promised to recruit settlers. While these speculative grants were later suspended, the first settlers who had been recruited and located in the townships were drawn from Loyalist sons and daughters and the growing tide of American land seekers—sometimes referred to as "late Loyalists". The two towns probably emerged out of this phase of settlement because they both had potential harbours and milling sites. The two towns and their surrounding townships continued to attract a steady flow of settlers through the first four decades of the century. Most of those who came during the 1820s and 1830s were from Britain—some being either military officers on half pay or minor landed gentry seeking to improve their fortunes. The influx of capital which accompanied these people, their landscape tastes, and predilection for mixed farming soon differentiated the area from others in the colony. English travellers passing through Cobourg and its environs looked approvingly at a town and countryside which they described as a comfortable, fashionable, prosperous place with a sense of society.

The back country, the townships to the north, were opened to settlers about 1818 when a group of retired naval and army officers occupied the north shore of Rice Lake.[3] The arrival of Peter Robinson's Irish emigrants in the mid-1820s paved the way for the opening of the interior and both Port Hope and Cobourg served as the points through which immigrants, supplies, and later the output of these new lands were directed. Strong social and economic links were forged between the towns on "the Front" and the frontier community around Peterborough.[4]

The first formal improvements in communications with the back country were undertaken very early in the settlement of the region. The earliest roads followed existing Indian trails. One in particular followed the ancient portage route connecting a point on the Ganaraska River about two miles upstream from Port Hope to the western end of Rice Lake. In 1818 an act was passed to improve this road to a width of forty feet and it is probable that for much of the road a new line was cut which better conformed to the survey system of the area. In later years this road was known variously as the east Gravel, Cavan or Peterborough Road, and it long remained the principal road artery to the back country from Port Hope.

Cobourg's road links to the back country were slower to develop. In 1825 Peter Robinson's settlers landed at Cobourg and cut a road north to Tidy's Tavern on Rice Lake at the present site of Gore's Landing.[5] In 1827 this road underwent further improvement said to have cost £600 which was borrowed by the magistrates from the Bank of Upper Canada.[6] Thereafter this road and at least two tributary roads, one to Sully (Harwood) and the other to connect with the Peterborough Road at Bewdley, provided links to the northern part of Cobourg's township hinterland and to the back country beyond Rice Lake. Between 1818 and 1827 several individuals petitioned for the right to operate ferries on Rice Lake to connect points on the south shore with those on the north shore and also the Trent and Otonabee Rivers.[7]

The decade of the 1830s ushered in a new phase in the development of the transportation structure of the area. Whereas most improvements in the early years of settlement had been sponsored and financed by local and provincial government, the initiative during the 1830s came increasingly from private interests. The *Cobourg Star* of May 31st 1831 announced a new stage coach service between Cobourg and Rice Lake, designed to link with east-west stage lines to York and Kingston. By 1833 there was a steam boat operating across Rice Lake to link the town of Peterborough and the head of the stage line from Cobourg.[8] By 1835 William Weller, the leading stage coach entrepreneur in Upper Canada and a resident of Cobourg, operated a stage line which linked Cobourg, Port Hope, and Peterborough.[9]

This new era of commercial stage and steam transportation had to cope with a system of roads of uniformly poor quality, and over which passage was slow and often impossible. The passage north out of Cobourg to Rice Lake, though only a distance of twelve miles, was by no means an easy one. Although much of the northern half of Hamilton Township was a sparsely wooded oak and pine plain where travel might be considered relatively easy, the problem was one of elevation, for the road had to surmount a summit seven hundred feet above the elevation of Cobourg. In many ways Port Hope's location was better suited to tapping the trade of the back country. This passage northward did not have to surmount as great an elevation over the morainic ridge but instead had the advantage of a saddle some two hundred feet lower in elevation than that of Cobourg's road. Moreover the line northward was not interrupted by Rice Lake and hence a direct passage to Peterborough and other points was possible.

The development of the transport infrastructure was not limited to road building. The two towns recognized the need to provide adequate connections to regional and international markets and suppliers. There had been east-west road connections from Port Hope and Cobourg to York and Kingston since the first years of occupance but bulk movement depended upon water transport on Lake Ontario. During the 1830s both towns wished to improve their facilities for landing boats in difficult weather. A substantial investment was therefore required to ensure the success of the trading and service aspirations of the local merchants. Accordingly joint stock companies were chartered in each town and efforts were made to improve the navigational and docking facilities of their harbours. By the 1840s both towns were serviced by packet steamers of the Royal Mail line which provided regular connections to such ports as Rochester, Kingston and Toronto.

The improvement of steamship connections on the Lakes in the 'forties was evidence that a new phase of transportation development was being ushered in, a phase that was responsive to the needs of a developing economy in the well established areas along Lake Ontario. The importance of reliable service connections with the townships of the back country also became apparent and the relative advantages offered by the two towns became more critical. If Port Hope had a natural advantage in its superior road connection to the back country, Cobourg had perhaps a slight advantage in the quality of its harbour. More important, however, was the fact that Cobourg had a significant population advantage over Port Hope throughout the first half century.[10]

The advantage was reflected in other ways. Throughout the 1840s Cobourg's exports exceeded those of its rival, and the number and variety of commercial and manufacturing establishments in Cobourg surpassed those of Port Hope. In particular, Cobourg's greater grist milling capacity and the large cloth factory employing nearly a hundred workers gave the town the appearance of economic dynamism not equalled by Port Hope. The leading investors of Cobourg must have regarded themselves as men of initiative and foresight, fully aware of the innovations in technology that were sweeping Britain. As early as 1831 a survey was carried out for a railway from Cobourg to Rice Lake, although a charter for this line was not obtained until early in 1834.[11] It is important to point out the boldness of this scheme, for it came at a time when the world's first operative railway was only five years old.[12] Undoubtedly not everyone shared this optimism, for the venture lapsed for the lack of capital. Guillet argues that the unsettled conditions surrounding the Rebellion of 1837 dampened enthusiam for business speculation. Whatever the reason, the idea of a railway did not surface again until the mid-1840s.

During the mid-'forties battle lines were being drawn between the two towns as each realized the prize to be won in controlling the back country.[13] R.D. Chatterton, editor of the *Cobourg Star* counselled:

. . . we would once more call attention to the Merchants and people of Cobourg to the imperative necessity that exists for their taking some immediate and effectual measures to establish a direct rail or plank road communication from this town to Peterboro! for unless they do this, and that as we say, immediately they will assuredly find themselves again forestalled, and the longer and more expensive route to Port Hope adopted to their irretrievable prejudice and disgrace.[14]

Cobourg's promoters responded to the call by proposing a planked road to the north. The dormant railway charter was revived in 1846 to be renamed the Cobourg and Rice Lake Plank Road and Ferry Company with William Weller as President. This road was built but after the second winter it had deteriorated badly and it is likely that many were loathe to pay tolls on such a poor road.

Not to be left behind, the people of Port Hope proposed and incorporated a company in 1846 to construct a railway between

Port Hope and Peterborough. But like the earlier railway proposed by Cobourg, the Port Hope company accomplished little before 1852. In all of these schemes the optimism of the local promoters fed more on fancy than on fact. It was felt that the improved line to the north would release a huge surplus of agricultural and forest produce which was building in the hinterland and which could not be exported by conventional means. Moreover the promoters assumed that the total trade of the back country would be moved by their particular line, and through their port to the exclusion of rival or alternative routes. The unbridled enthusiasm of the promoters knew no restraint.

> . . . such a line which would connect with the proposed Toronto and Kingston Railroad would establish Cobourg at once and forever as a central and most important station—the natural outlet and port for the whole trade of the richest and most extensive range of back country probably in all Canada . . . . in comparison with the ultimate value of which the cost of the proposed work would be literally nothing—a drop of water in a mine of gold.[15]

Meanwhile Port Hope promoters, without benefit of prior experience, nor as yet even a survey of the proposed route, felt confident enough to announce a schedule of passenger fares and freight rates which would apply to their line.[16]

The enthusiasm of Cobourg's citizens for improving communications was not dampened by the failure of the plank road. With the government's implementation of the Railway Guarantee Act of 1849, and a succession of good harvests thereafter, the stage was set for another railway proposal. In November 1852, the Cobourg and Peterborough Railway Company was incorporated and a route envisioned which would cross Rice Lake by means of a causeway. For this venture the citizens of Cobourg subscribed £125,000.[17]

When the Cobourg and Peterborough Railway was initiated, the promoters of the Port Hope and Peterborough Railway reacted by changing their route to terminate at Lindsay rather than Peterborough, and obtained authority to build through to Beaverton on Lake Simcoe. The name of the line was changed accordingly to the Port Hope, Lindsay and Beaverton Railway. The line obtained $920,000 in municipal bonuses to start construction. [18]

In the race to complete lines to the interior, the Cobourg and Peterborough Railway arrived first, reaching Peterborough at the end of 1855. However this was only accomplished after agonizing delays and disputes with the contractor, and the anxiety to complete the line quickly proved costly. Engineering studies had been poorly executed with the result that the gradient of the road over the summit of the interlobate moraine reduced the hauling capacity of trains to ten percent of normal. Furthermore, miscalculation of the depth of Rice Lake made a causeway unfeasible and a bridge had to be substituted. However the piers of the bridge were inadequately anchored and part of the structure was carried away by ice during the first winter and had to be replaced. Thus began what was to be a sequence of financial set backs which spanned the next thirty-three years. The chronicle of difficulty is too long to recite here, and suffice to say, the line never proved to be a financial success. By 1860, Cobourg's citizens had invested upwards of one million dollars in a line which was in danger of becoming derelict. [19] The line had achieved one of its objectives: it did provide a means of moving the increasing output of the Peterborough region. Traffic over the line peaked in 1856, the second year of operation, when nearly sixteen million board feet of lumber, fifty-seven thousand bushels of wheat and twenty thousand barrels of flour were shipped to Cobourg from Peterborough. [20] Undoubtedly, the net benefits of the line fell to the producers of the back country rather than to the promoters of the line. When the Port Hope line was finally open as far as Millbrook, and when it appeared certain that the Cobourg line was a folly, a branch line to connect the Port Hope, Lindsay and Beaverton Railway to Peterborough was proposed and later built. By 1858, Peterborough was linked by rail to Port Hope and it is clear that back country shippers had no problems of conscience in choosing between lines.

Port Hope may have lost the race to the back country but it clearly won the struggle for control of the trade. In fact the Port Hope line achieved financial success, something that many other short "feeder" lines in Canada failed to do. Every year traffic and revenues over the line showed an increase. As early as 1864 the line had sufficient surplus cash to buy the Port Hope Harbour Company.[21] By 1869, further expansion was contemplated and the name of the line was changed to the Midland Railway Company of Canada. Plans were laid to push the line through to Georgian Bay in pursuit of the westward moving lumber frontier.[22]

Meanwhile, Cobourg's ill-fated line was bouncing from bankruptcy to new and greater folly under new ownership. Efforts were made to link the line to an iron mine at Marmora, thirty-five miles east of Peterborough. Unfortunately the problem of crossing Rice Lake continued to cause interruptions and uncertainty in service and the quality of the iron mines proved disappointing.

The most remarkable feature of the life of the Cobourg line is the irrepressible appetite on the part of the citizens of that community for further development and investment in their railway. By the time the line was finally given up as a failure in 1889 the town had accumulated an enormous debt and it would have been larger had the provincial government not cancelled the principal of the debt to the Municipal Loan Fund.[23] It should be noted that Port Hope was given a similar exemption.

The decade of the 1860s which had started with such expectation of civic grandeur for Cobourg proved to be a period of financial collapse. There can be no greater symbol of the optimism of Cobourg's citizens than the monumental Court House—opened with great ceremony by the Prince of Wales in 1860. Yet, no sooner was the Court House opened than it was found there was no money to pay the contractor. In fact, it was not until 1938 that the citizens of Cobourg finally paid the debt on their Court House.[24] It is of some interest to note that some of the prominent men of Cobourg shifted their money and leadership to the Port Hope based line soon after it was discovered that the Cobourg venture was going to be unsuccessful. Men like D'Arcy Boulton and Henry Covert, long associated with a variety of interests in Cobourg, including the Cobourg and Peterborough Railway, surface as principal shareholders in the Midland Railway in the late 1860s. In all probability, these men lost little from the collapse of the Cobourg line; indeed Guillet notes that the principal advocates of that line profiteered on the sale of land for the right of way.[25]

By the mid 1860s, Cobourg's dreams of becoming the outlet for the Peterborough region were destroyed. Port Hope was in the ascendancy. The gap in population between the two towns began to close. Cobourg did not disappear nor even decline in size, but growth tended to stagnate. Undoubtedly, many of Cobourg's citizens suffered financial set-backs and may have felt themselves victims of a cruel fate. But what was this fate? Was it simply that their town was located in such a way that an unbridgeable lake interposed itself between them and their anticipated hinterland? In the absence of better technical advice they had invested heavily in a poor solution for overcoming this barrier. But poor planning and bad management had not dampened the enthusiasm which set the railroad venture in motion. More important is the question of how this town and surrounding rural community of only six or seven thousand people could embark on such an optimistic and costly venture?

In the vast expanse of new land which was British North America during the first half of the nineteenth century it is not surprising that men developed a sense of identity with a local community or local urban centre. Just as the creation and development of new towns overnight fascinates modern twentieth century observers, it must surely have inspired nineteenth century men. By the middle decade of that century, Upper Canadians were surrounded by evidence of the great material advancement of their colony and of themselves, and they accordingly came to equate these dramatic changes with the "doctrine of success or progress".[26]

The central assumptions of the doctrine were that change and improvement are one and the same, and are purposeful —leading to ever increasing levels of material and social well-being. Moreover progress was contingent upon human agency. Man could, through the power of his will and intelligence, and hard work, produce continuous growth in the social patrimony. In Upper Canada, the idea of progress was inextricably tied to agriculture. The farmer, the sturdy yeoman, toiling endlessly to clear the land, was seen to be the standard-bearer of progress. This notion filtered down to the Upper Canadian farmer and gave him a sense of his own dignity and generated hope that his efforts would be rewarded. Hope was sustained by the evidence around him that material progress was indeed occurring. Thus it was that the idea of progress became almost universally accepted by Upper Canadians by 1850. With it came a faith in the future, and this secular faith came to be proclaimed with a vigour and enthusiasm akin to the emotional outpourings that characterized their religious faith.

This faith was shared by the small town merchants and artisans, most of whom were dependent upon the success of the agricultural sector of the province's economy. So it was that the citizens of Cobourg and Port Hope could confidently launch their respective improvement schemes. The doctrine of progress gave assurance that their bold and aggressive action would be rewarded, and moreover by improving links with the back country they were providing the means whereby the farmer could reap the reward of his drudgery. One of the fundamental principles of Upper Canadian political economic theory at mid-century was that improved links between the Front and the interior would make wild lands of the back country more valuable. This assumption provided the basis of government participation in the funding of these railways and certainly must have motivated those Tory squires who owned large acreages of wild lands to acquiesce in what might have been an otherwise unpalatable undertaking.[27]

For the citizens of Cobourg, the realization of the folly of their hope of becoming the trade outlet of the region was slow to register. The doctrine of progress was a powerful ideology and evidence of material advance continued to be amassed as the country under Confederation marched westward. However, at the local level the geography of Southern Ontario was changing rapidly during the second half of the nineteenth century. Toronto emerged as the dominant metropolis of the region and its influence in controlling the trade of a number of local hinterlands along the shores of Lake Ontario became increasingly obvious. By the 1880s, local feeder railways were being absorbed by larger "national" lines and local men no longer exercised the corporate control they once did. Many towns across the province finding themselves by-passed by railways or unable to compete with larger centres lapsed into a period of protracted stagnation or decline. The irony of the era was that it provided a lesson on the single most important characteristic of Canada's geographical condition—the need to overcome distance. Canadians did begin to learn that there were very great costs involved in being a small number of people in a large land, just as they began to learn that the resources of Canada were different from those of the United States and that the strategy for exploiting these resources must necessarily be suited to this different environment. But these lessons were learned slowly and in the process there were many ''Cobourgs'' where hopes of grandeur were made to face a crushing reality.

Notes

[1]*Canadian Agricultural Journal*, i, 1844, p. 40.

[2]E.C. Guillet, *The Valley of the Trent* (Toronto: Champlain Society, 1957), p. 138.

[3]Entry to these townships beyond the ''Front'' was made possible by a Crown land purchase from the Mississauga Indians in November of 1818 and May 1819. The military officers became settlers because the Rush-Bagot Agreement of 1818 limited the military armament on the Great Lakes thereby causing a demobilization of some British forces.

[4]This assertion goes beyond the obvious service role the towns played for the interior settlements. A cursory survey of the land holdings and business activity of leading citizens such as Zacheus Burnham, John G. Bethune and George S. Boulton and others suggests that Cobourg (and perhaps Port Hope) played an important part in the development of the hinterland generally and towns like Peterborough particularly. Much of their activity involved land speculation, but some merchants opened branch operations and others appear to have dispatched agents or members of their family to the back country to oversee their affairs, thereby creating a network of interests throughout the region. The full extent to which group movement and/or business interests in older communities on the Front fostered new communities in the back country remains to be investigated for Upper Canada.

[5]The Honourable Peter Robinson's Report, 1827, in Guillet, . . . *Trent*, *op. cit.*, p. 123. Robinson stated that the road north from Cobourg was hardly passable and that with a grant of £50 from the local magistrates and the labour of his Irish immigrants improvements were made so that wagons could reach Rice Lake.

[6]Mr. John Smith, Junr., Deputy Provincial Surveyor, General Account of the Newcastle District, 1827, in Guillet, . . . *Trent*, *op. cit.*, p. 31.

[7]Public Archives of Canada, R.G. 1, E3, Vol. 26.

[8]*Cobourg Star*, July 31, 1833.

[9]E.C. Guillet, *Cobourg, 1798-1948* (Oshawa, 1948), p. 65.

[10]In spite of a very rapid rate of growth during the 1840s Port Hope still trailed Cobourg in population by 1851. The Census of that year credits Cobourg with a population of 3,871 compared to 2,476 in Port Hope.

[11]Guillet, . . . *Trent*, *op. cit.*, p. lii.

[12]Guillet, *Cobourg*. . . , *op. cit.*, p. 71. Cobourg was not alone in this "early" railway speculation. In the southwestern part of Ontario alone there were seventeen separate petitions for railway charters before 1840. See J.J. Talman, "The Development of the Railway Network of Southwestern Ontario to 1876", *Historical Papers*, Canadian Historical Association, 1953, p. 53.

[13]The newspapers of the towns give little indication of open rivalry before 1845. Undoubtedly Cobourg's civic successes in the form of Victoria College, the Court House, the well known Albion Hotel, the presence of luminaries like William Weller and a very well placed corps of Tory squires, would have been cause for envy on the part of Port Hope's promoters.

[14]*Cobourg Star*, December 17, 1845.

[15]*Cobourg Star*, July 25, 1846.

[16]A.W. Currie, *The Grand Trunk Railway of Canada* (Toronto, 1957), p. 281.

[17]This is a remarkable sum when one realizes that the assessed value of property for Cobourg and Hamilton township in 1847 was just under £64,000.

[18]Currie, *op. cit.*, p. 281.

[19]G.R. Stevens, *Canadian National Railways*, Vol. I (Toronto, 1960), p. 431.

[20]Guillet, . . . *Trent*, *op. cit.*, p. 253.

[21]Stevens, *op. cit.*, p. 436.

[22]*Ibid.*, p. 436-7.

[23]Guillet, *Cobourg* . . . , *op. cit.*, p. 101.

[24]*Ibid.*, p. 100.

[25]*Ibid.*, p. 74.

[26]The doctrine of progress as it applies to Upper Canada is the subject of a thesis by Lawrence S. Fallis, Jr., "The Idea of Progress in the Province of Canada: 1841-1867", unpublished Ph.D., University of Michigan, 1966. I have used this thesis as the basis of the discussion which follows.

[27]Fallis argues that Tories might be one group among the Canadian population who would be opposed to the doctrine since it implied that change, growth and development were essential to the welfare of the nation. Fallis, *op. cit.*, p. 31-2.

Part III:
Epilogue and
Bibliography

11. EPILOGUE

David Wood

> . . . this is an age of progress . . . the tide of population and
> production which is destined to flow over and to fill the
> several channels of communication as they are successively
> opened up, is rising higher and higher on every side. . . . it
> would seem to be . . . the part of true wisdom to look with
> much confidence to the future, and to take due account of
> advantages which, although they be prospective, are by no
> means problematical. (Lord Elgin, at sod-turning, Ontario
> Simcoe and Huron Railroad, from *The Globe*, 16th Oct.
> 1851)

By the middle of the nineteenth century a distinctive aura had
arisen in Upper Canada, an aura of optimism which was shared
with the neighbour to the south. This is the point at which most
of the essays in this book draw to a close. It is beyond the first
generation of settlement; Griffith Taylor likely would have
called it the adolescent stage. This is the opening of the railway
era in Upper Canada when, according to the Mayor of Toronto
in his introduction of Lord Elgin at the sod-turning in October,
1851, the railways would tap "resources for profitable enterprise, to which it would be difficult . . . to assign a limit". This
book has paid little attention to the railway network which began
expanding in the 1850s. It was to cause fundamental re-
adjustments in economic strategies and thereby in many of the
details of settlement. It will be recalled that some of the essays

probe into the second half of the nineteenth century, but essentially the era of this book is pre-railway.

By 1850 the appearances of prosperity had become common in south-central Canada West. Lord Elgin referred to "the fertility and capabilities of the country" adjacent to Yonge Street. We have spoken about the early "landscape of change"; although the rate of change probably was not lessened, after mid-century the appellation "landscape of progress"—in the full meaning of that term—might be applied. The progress meant a number of things that have become associated with the frontier: a fading of imported class distinctions, success in agricultural establishment and related industry, significant improvements in roads and canals, growing sophistication in urban services and architecture, development of a public system of education, and the appearance of a Canadian political identity including a larger degree of autonomy in governance. But more than this, progress meant a passionate belief in growth, so much so that it was often next to impossible to distinguish a reform from a conservative newspaper on the topic of the rightness of municipal indebtedness for the purposes of "progress". Ontario came to be the embodiment of its "contending allegiances", through what had become a kind of working arrangement: quickened by an American initiative, but clothed with British administrative and legislative traditions. J.W. Watson (in *North America,* p. 230) has described it as a marrying of "European styles with American needs, something distinctive".

Southern Ontario was not, of course, an isotropic plain either physiographically or socially. One would expect, therefore, to find in it contrasts as well as comparisons. The concept of progress obviously meant something different to the Old Order Mennonites, and it was not adhered to with passion by the Irish Catholics of Douro and adjacent townships. There were different degrees of political radicalism and dissidence across the colony, and there was a variable distribution of forfeited estates. Speculation seems to have been a frontier phenomenon that was common in most districts; mapping of it for different periods would be revealing. The proto-urban nucleations appear to have arranged themselves into networks, although even in periods of relative economic stability there were numerous exceptions to Christaller's theoretical pattern of a triangular lattice of urban centres in a plane of hexagonal market areas.[1] Perhaps for the parts of southern Ontario touched by Simcoe's plan an alternative construct is more apropos. An obvious example is Whebell's system of corridors; his case study is based on the military roads and urban nuclei bestowed by Simcoe on Upper Canada, which were re-inforced through various changes in economy and organization and are reflected even in the modern urban network.[2] The debate over the question of the diffusion *vs* the invention of innovations, and modifications to them, will have an important place in the increasing understanding of Ontario's past, not least in the investigation of cultural transfer. Some broader implications of this present collection of essays lie in the comparisons of frontiers: the Upper Canada story has much to gain from documentation of frontiers in western Canada, the United States, and perhaps Australia, and of course much to give.

The questions to be answered are legion, and the asking, the interpreting and re-interpreting will go on from one generation of answers to its successors. The bibliography that follows is designed to be of service to the inquiring reader who wishes to begin pursuit through relevant, readily-available sources. The number of items included has been kept modest; in most cases the references shown will lead to numerous others, as will the footnotes of the essays in the present volume.

Notes

[1]*Cf* John U. Marshall, "Central Places in the Queen's Bush: a Study of Service Centres and their Evolution in Bruce and Grey Counties, Ontario", unpub. M.A. thesis, University of Minnesota, 1964.

[2]C.F.J. Whebell, "Corridors: a Theory of Urban Systems", *Annals*, Association of American Geographers, 59 (Mar. 1969), pp. 1-26.

12. SOME REFERENCES ON THE HISTORICAL GEOGRAPHY OF UPPER CANADA

There are a few works, to which most of us are indebted, which cover broad topics in Ontario's past. Most of these are found in the "Context" list. In that same list the reader will find items which allow comparisons between the geographical patterns of the past in Ontario and those in related areas. The references are divided according to subject matter, reflecting the essays in the book. The essays are not mutually exclusive and neither are the references suggested here; where duplication occurs, it should be understood that the reference is to a different part of the work. This basic bibliography is offered as an adjunct to the essays, and it is recommended that the footnotes throughout the volume also be consulted.

A context for Upper Canada and its settlement

J.B. Brebner
1945   *North Atlantic Triangle/The Interplay of Canada, The United States and Great Britain*, New York, Columbia Univ. Press; Carleton Library edition, with introduction by D.G. Creighton, 1966.
J.M.S. Careless
1967   *The Union of the Canadas/The Growth of Canadian Institutions 1841-1857*, The Canadian Centenary Series, Toronto, McClelland and Stewart.
A.H. Clark
1949   *The Invasion of New Zealand by People, Plants and Animals: The South Island*, New Brunswick, N.J., Rutgers University.

1959   *Three Centuries and the Island/A Historical Geography of Settlement and Agriculture in Prince Edward Island, Canada*, Univ. of Toronto Press.

G.M. Craig
1963   *Upper Canada/The Formative Years/1784-1841*, The Canadian Centenary Series, Toronto, McClelland and Stewart.

M.S. Cross
1970   (ed.) *The Frontier Thesis and the Canadas: The Debate on the Impact of the Canadian Environment*, Issues in Canadian History . . . , Toronto, Copp Clark. A collection of fundamental readings both descriptive and interpretive. Others in the series are relevant.
1974   (ed.) *The Workingman in the Nineteenth Century*, Toronto, Oxford University Press. One of a new series of books of readings on Canadian history. The selections are engrossing as well as instructive.

W.T. Easterbrook and M.H. Watkins
1967   *Approaches to Canadian Economic History*, a selection of essays edited and with an introduction by W.T.E. and M.H.W., the Carleton Library No. 31, Toronto, McClelland & Stewart.

A. Gowans
1966   *Building Canada/an architectural history of Canadian life*, Toronto, Oxford University Press.

R.C. Harris
1967   "Historical Geography", *The Canadian Geographer*, xi, pp 235-250. A review of the accomplishments and the tasks ahead, with a thorough bibliography including theses.

R.C. Harris and J. Warkentin
1974   *Canada Before Confederation/A Study in Historical Geography*, New York, Oxford University Press.

J.T. Lemon
1972   *The Best Poor Man's Country/A Geographical Study of Early Southeastern Pennsylvania*, Baltimore, Johns Hopkins.

T.H. Levere and R.A. Jarrell
1974   *A Curious Field-book/Science and Society in Canadian*

History, Toronto, Oxford University Press. Readings (*cf* Cross, 1974).

Bruce Sinclair, N.R. Ball, J.O. Petersen
1974   (eds.) *Let Us Be Honest and Modest/Technology and Society in Canadian History*, Toronto, Oxford University Press. Readings (*cf* Cross, 1974).

J. Warkentin
1968   *Canada/A Geographical Interpretation*, auspices of Canadian Association of Geographers, edited by J.W., Toronto, Methuen. Especially Parts I & II, and chapter 11.

J. Wreford Watson
1963   *North America/Its Countries and Regions*, London, Longmans, Green. Especially chapters 6,7,8,10,12.

Prehistorical settlement

C.E. Heidenreich
1971   *Huronia/A History and Geography of the Huron Indians, 1600-1650*, Toronto, McClelland and Stewart.

W.A. Kenyon
1968   "The Miller Site", *Royal Ontario Museum, Art and Archaeology Occasional Paper*, No. 14.

V.A. Konrad
1973   *The Archaeological Resources of the Metropolitan Toronto Planning Area: Inventory and Prospect*, Department of Geography, York University Discussion Paper, No. 10.

B.G. Trigger
1970   "The Strategy of Iroquoian Prehistory", *Ontario Archaeology*, No. 14, pp. 3-48.

J.V. Wright
1966   "The Ontario Iroquois Tradition", *National Museum of Canada Bulletin*, No. 210.
1972   *Ontario Prehistory*, National Museum of Man, National Museums of Canada.

A military colony in a wilderness

W.H. Bartlett
1968   *Bartlett's Canada/A Pre-Confederation Journey*, introduction by Henry C. Campbell, Toronto, McClelland & Stewart. Includes all the Canadian engravings of W.H.B.
Michael Bell
1973   *Painters in a New Land*, Toronto.
M.S. Cross
1970   (ed.) *The Frontier Thesis and the Canadas . . .* , Toronto, Copp Clark. Readings (see full reference above).
R.L. Gentilcore
1972   (ed.) *Ontario*, Studies in Canadian Geography, Univ. of Toronto Press.
C.P. Lucas
1912   *Lord Durham's Report on the Affairs of British North America*, edited with an introduction by C.P.L., in three volumes, Oxford, Clarendon Press. Reprinted 1970 by A.M. Kelley, New York (facsimile).
D.W. Meinig
1971   *Southwest/Three Peoples in Geographical Change, 1600-1700*, New York, Oxford Univ. Press. A stimulating reconstruction of another area which found itself a borderland of the expanding United States.
Anne Wilkinson
1956   *Lions in the Way*, Toronto, Macmillan. One example of the accounts written by gentry, in this case referring to the ministry of the Oslers in the back country around Bond Head (from 1830s).

Transportation in the landscape of early Upper Canada

The transportation landscape of Upper Canada is a subject for which one develops a feeling by reading contemporary and modern accounts of the settling experience; particular sources closely focused on the subject do not exist. A few of the most useful recent works are listed below.

C.H. Danhof
1969   *Change in Agriculture*, Cambridge, Massachusetts.
        This very perceptive account of the day-by-day process
        of farmmaking and farm operation has many sidelights
        on neighbourhood mobility and marketing procedures.
L.F. Gates
1968   *Land Policies of Upper Canada*, Toronto. Local access
        is shown to be an important subject of consideration in
        the complex sequence of plans and modified plans for
        public land disposal in Upper Canada.
G.P. Glazebrook
1964   *A History of Transportation in Canada*, rev. ed., To-
        ronto. Long the basic work on the subject in Canada this
        book emphasizes characteristics of modes and changes
        in them.
E.C. Guillet
1966   *The Story of Canadian Roads*, Toronto. This illustrated,
        anecdotal treatment conveys the spirit of inland travel in
        early Ontario.
T.F. McIlwraith
1970   "The Adequacy of Rural Roads in the Era before Rail-
        ways: An Illustration from Upper Canada", *The Cana-
        dian Geographer*, 14, pp. 344-360. This paper discus-
        ses the utilization of the Ontario system of road allow-
        ances, based upon evidence of farming activity.

Impact of agricultural settlement on the land

As with Transportation, there is little in an accessible published
form dealing with early agriculture in Ontario. The following
list is designed chiefly to allow a reader to pursue the topic as it
applies to comparable areas.

P.W. Bidwell and J.I. Falconer
1925   *History of Agriculture in the Northern United States,
        1620-1860*, Washington, Carnegie Institution.
I. Bowman
1937   (ed.) *The Limits of Land Settlement*, New York, Coun-
        cil on Foreign Relations. This was preceded by two

other related works, *Pioneer Problems* (1932) and *The Pioneer Fringe* (1931), under the auspices of the American Geographical Society.

Andrew H. Clark
1959 *Three Centuries and the Island . . .* , Univ. of Toronto Press. See full reference above.

V.C. Fowke
1946 *Canadian Agricultural Policy*, Univ. of Toronto Press.

G.V. Jacks and R.O. Whyte
1939 *The Rape of the Earth*, London, Faber & Faber.

Robert Leslie Jones
1946 *History of Agriculture in Ontario/1613-1880*, Univ. of Toronto Press.

Kenneth Kelly
1973 "Notes on a Type of Mixed Farming Practised in Ontario During the Early Nineteenth Century", *The Canadian Geographer*, XVII No. 3, pp. 205-219.

D.A. Lawr
1972 "The Development of Ontario Farming, 1870-1914: Patterns of Growth and Change", *Ontario History*, LXIV, pp. 239-251.

Bruce Sinclair, N.R. Ball, J.O. Petersen
1974 *Let Us Be Honest and Modest Technology and Society in Canadian History*, Toronto, Oxford Univ. Press. Readings; especially sections 2 and 4.

William L. Thomas
1956 *Man's Role in Changing the Face of the Earth*, Univ. of Chicago Press.

Forest exploitation

A.R.M. Lower
1936 *Settlement and the Forest Frontier in Eastern Canada*, with Innis on mining in Vol. IX, Canadian Frontiers of Settlement series, Toronto, Macmillan.

1938 *The North American Assault on the Canadian Forest*: a history of the lumber trade between Canada and the U.S. . . . , Toronto, Ryerson, for the Carnegie Endowment for International Peace.

1973 *Great Britain's Woodyard; British America and the*

timber trade, 1763-1867, Montreal, McGill-Queen's Univ. Press.

Contrasts in Shield/non-Shield settlement

L.J. Chapman and D.F. Putnam
1966   *The Physiography of Southern Ontario*, 2nd edition, Univ. of Toronto Press.
L.F. Gates
1968   *Land Policies of Upper Canada*, Canadian Studies in History and Government, No. 9, Univ. of Toronto Press.
E.C. Guillet
1933   *Early Life in Upper Canada*, Univ. of Toronto Press.
1963   *The Pioneer Farmer and Backwoodsman* (2 vols), Univ. of Toronto Press.
1957   *The Valley of the Trent*, The Champlain Society, University of Toronto Press.
Norman Macdonald
1939   *Canada, 1763-1841, Immigration and Settlement: The Administration of Imperial Land Regulations*, London, Longmans, Green.
J.E. Middleton and F. Landon
1927   *The Province of Ontario—A History, 1615-1927*, Toronto.
G.C. Paterson
1921   "Land Settlement in Upper Canada, 1783-1840", Government of Ontario, Department of Archives, *Sixteenth Annual Report, 1920*.

The Canada Company and settlement as resource development

James M. Cameron
1966   "Guelph and the Canada Company, 1827-1851—An Approach to Resource Development", Unpublished M. Sc. thesis, University of Guelph.

S.D. Clark
1968 *The Developing Canadian Community*, 2nd Edition, Toronto, University of Toronto Press.

H.I. Cowan
1961 *British Emigration to British North America: The First Hundred Years*, Revised Edition, Toronto, University of Toronto Press.

William Dunlop
1967 *Tiger Dunlop's Upper Canada*, Introduction by Carl F. Klinck, Toronto, McClelland and Stewart.

W.T. Easterbrook and Hugh G.J. Aitken
1956 *Canadian Economic History*, Toronto, Macmillan.

Norman Macdonald
1939 *Canada, 1763-1841: Immigration and Settlement*, London. Full reference above.

G.C. Paterson
1921 "Land Settlement in Upper Canada, 1783-1840", Ontario Archives, *Sixteenth Annual Report, 1920*, Toronto.

H.A. Stevenson, and F.H. Armstrong
1969 (contributing eds.) *Approaches to Teaching Local History Using Upper Canadian and Ontario Examples*, Toronto, Oxford University Press.

Urban progress and decline (especially Kingston)

J.M. Gilmour
1972 *Spatial Evolution of Manufacturing: Southern Ontario 1851- 1891*, Dep't of Geography Research Publications, Univ. of Toronto Press.

P.G. Goheen
1970 *Victorian Toronto, 1850-1900: Pattern and Process of Growth*, Dep't of Geography Research Paper No. 127, Univ. of Chicago.

D.C. Masters
1947 *The Rise of Toronto 1850-1890*, Univ. of Toronto Press.

R. A. Preston
1959 *Kingston Before the War of 1812, A collection of*

documents, The Champlain Society, Univ. of Toronto Press.

J. Spelt
1972   *Urban Development in South-Central Ontario*, The Carleton Library No. 57, Toronto, McClelland & Stewart (original edition, 1955).

G. Tulchinsky
1976   (ed.) *Kingston in the Nineteenth Century: essays on social and economic change in a minor metropolis*, Montreal, McGill-Queen's Univ. Press (forthcoming).

Ideology and inter-urban competition (especially Cobourg and Pt Hope)

A.W. Currie
1957   *The Grand Trunk Railway of Canada*, Toronto.

Lawrence S. Fallis, Jr.
1968   "The Idea of Progress in the Province of Canada: a study in the History of Ideas", in *The Shield of Achilles; aspects of Canada in the Victorian Age*, W.L. Morton, ed., Toronto. This essay is useful but for a more complete examination of the Idea of Progress, see Fallis' thesis cited in footnote 26, chapter 10 *(supra)*.

E.C. Guillet
1948   *Cobourg, 1798-1948*. Oshawa.
1957   *The Valley of the Trent*, The Champlain Society, Univ. of Toronto Press. This volume is one of a series published by the Champlain Society which makes available important primary source materials.
1966   *The Story of Canadian Roads*, Toronto. This is a rather anecdotal volume but contains some technical information.

Thomas C. Keefer
1972   *The Philosophy of Railroads and other Essays*, H.V. Nelles, ed., Toronto. This volume is a reprint of Keefer's essay first published in 1850. Nelles provides

an excellent essay on the context of railway development in Canada.

G.R. Stevens

1960   *Canadian National Railways*, 2 vols., Toronto.

J.J. Talman

1953   ''The Development of the Railway Network of Southwestern Ontario to 1876'', *Historical Papers*, Canadian
Historical Association.

LIST OF CONTRIBUTORS

ALAN BRUNGER was born near Swindon, England in 1942. He graduated from the University of Southampton with a B.Sc., in 1963. After emigrating to Canada in 1964 he completed a M.Sc. at the University of Alberta at Calgary in 1966 and received a Ph.D. from the University of Western Ontario in 1974. He became an Assistant Professor in the Department of Geography at Trent University in 1969 where he has taught for five years. He is engaged in research on the historical settlement geography of Southern Ontario and is particularly interested in the pattern of response of individual settlers to official schemes of colonization in the nineteenth century.

JAMES M. CAMERON has a B.A. (Hons.) from the University of Western Ontario, M.Sc. from the University of Guelph and his Ph.D. from the University of Glasgow. His current research interests are Scottish emigration to Upper Canada, and Brewing industry in Ontario during the 19th century. He is an associate professor in geography and, until recently, was associate dean of Atkinson College, York University.

PETER ENNALS studied at the University of Toronto and taught at Queen's University before joining the faculty of Mount Allison University. He has done research on 19th century rural architecture in Ontario and settlement in the Newcastle District of Upper Canada.

R. LOUIS GENTILCORE has taught historical geography at McMaster University for over a decade. He took his bachelor's studies at the University of Toronto and then completed his doctorate at the University of Maryland in 1950. His general research activities come under the title Geographical change in Upper Canada, and at present he is preparing (with Grant Head) a facsimile atlas with commentary dealing primarily with nineteenth century Ontario.

C. GRANT HEAD holds a B.A. and M.A. from McMaster University, and a Ph.D. from the University of Wisconsin, Madison, and is currently an assistant professor of Wilfrid Laurier University at Waterloo, Ontario. His continuing research interest is in the patterns, processes and effects of the exploitation of Canada's staple resources, particularly the Newfoundland fisheries of the eighteenth century and the Ontario forests of the nineteenth century.

KENNETH KELLY, Associate Professor and Chairman of Geography, University of Guelph, B.A. and M.A. Leeds, Ph.D., Toronto. Major research topics—Geography of 19th century rural Ontario, especially the inter-relationships between agricultural settlers and the physical environment, and the evolution of agriculture; British influences on the intensification of agriculture (Ph.D. thesis and 9 published papers on these topics).

VICTOR A. KONRAD has B.A. and M.A. degrees from York University, and is presently a Ph.D. candidate at McMaster University. He has recently directed a government-sponsored emergency survey of prehistorical sites in Metro Toronto and environs. His current research interests include prehistorical resource appreciation and terrain adjustment and prehistorical settlement, in the Toronto area, and Iroquois villages on the north shore of Lake Ontario (1665-1687).

THOMAS F. MCILWRAITH has an M.A. from the University of Toronto (local access in York County, Ontario), and a Ph.D. from Wisconsin (the logistics of the Great Lakes grain trade, focusing on dimensions and carrying capabilities of boats, canals, etc.). He has a continuing interest in agricultural and transportation change in the development of North America from the 17th to the 19th century. He is presently assistant professor in Geography at Erindale College, University of Toronto.

BRIAN S. OSBORNE received his B.A. from the University of Southampton in 1960, and his Ph.D. from that institution in 1967. He taught at Southern Colorado State College from 1963 to 1967, and since that date he has been at Queen's University in Kingston, where he is an Associate Professor in the Geography

Department. His present research activities come under the general heading of frontier settlement in eighteenth and nineteenth century Ontario.

JOHN DAVID WOOD began his university studies at Memorial University of Newfoundland, and completed his B.A. and M.A. at the University of Toronto. His doctoral studies, which arose out of an interest in the migration of Scots and their life-styles from their homeland to the New World, were carried out at Edinburgh University. He has taught at Edinburgh, Alberta and York Universities. His current research pursuit is to assess frontiers in comparative terms, especially within Canada.

INDEX